SKI CAMPING

by Ron Watters
photographs by Phil Schofield

Happy Skiing! To our good son and fine friend, Dan. Xmas 1981 Dad & Mom

A Solstice Press Book

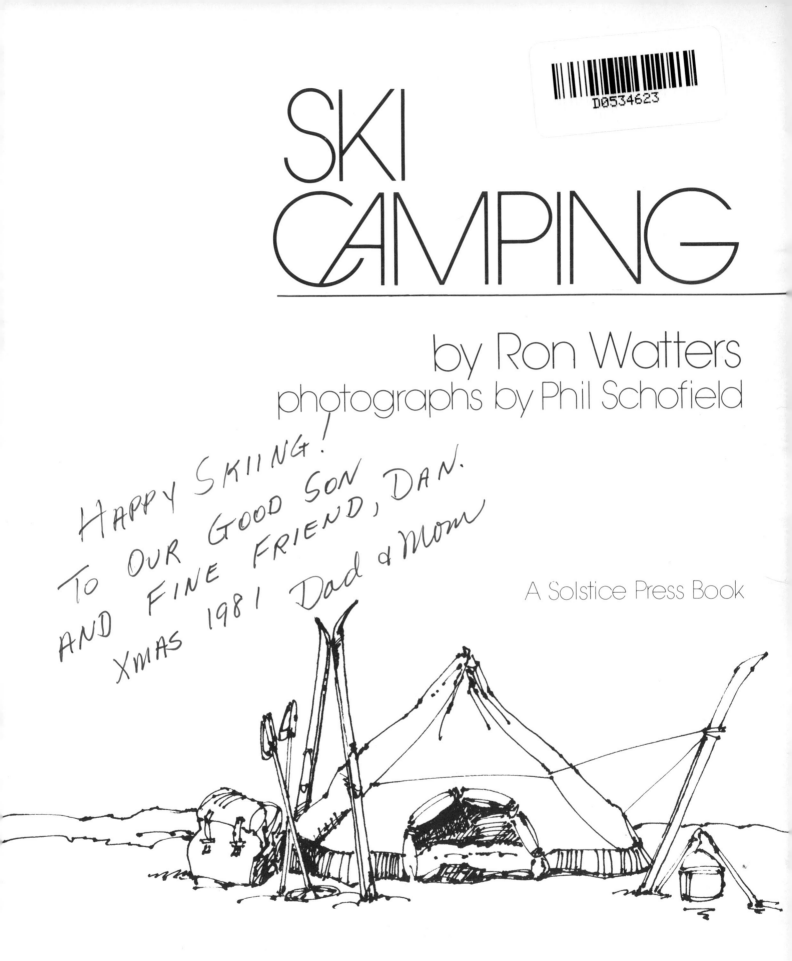

Chronicle Books   San Francisco

In Memory of John Merriam

and those precious campfire evenings
when he sat and chewed and shared his
stories, wisdom and love for the wild,
untrammeled backcountry which he
fought hard to protect for all of us.

The photos of snow crystals on page 141
are from the *Field Guide to Snow Crystals*
by Ed LaChapelle and are used with
permission of the University of
Washington Press.

© 1979 by North Country Book Express, Inc.

A Solstice Press Book produced at North
Country Book Express, Moscow, Idaho, by
Dana Sloan and Bob Jebb under the
direction of Ivar Nelson and Patricia Hart.

Library of Congress Cataloging in Publication Data

Watters, Ron.
    Ski Camping.

    1. Snow Camping.   2. Cross-country.
I. Title.
GV198.9.W37   796.5'4   79-22843

ISBN 0-87701-165-6

Chronicle Books
870 Market Street
San Francisco, California 94102

Preface

This is a book to help you keep warm and comfortable while skiing and camping in the backcountry. It is also a book about self-reliance. In the winter backcountry, self-reliance means being prepared with the right equipment and right clothing. But more important, it means good judgment and being responsible for one's own decisions.

Unlike downhill ski areas, which have carefully groomed ski runs and a well trained ski patrol ready to help at a moments notice, the backcountry has neither groomed trails nor assistance on call. Nor is it wanted. Part of the adventure and the excitement that draws people to the wilds is the unknown, the uncertainty and the risk.

The backcountry is one place where you are in control of, and responsible for, your own safety. In the winter, the power of nature commands our respect. Heed that command, and the winter wilderness will show all of its glory and beauty.

Some people have recently proposed the closing of popular backcountry areas because avalanche hazard exists. We will rue the day that ever happens, for one of the great freedoms of the wilderness, the freedom to seek adventure, will be lost.

Let's fight to protect our wild areas, work to minimize our impact on them, and battle to keep them the way they are — wild, dangerous, uncertain, risky and free.

Ron Watters
August 1979
Mouth of the South Fork, Idaho

Acknowledgments

This book is the result of the combined energy and enthusiasm of many people. Behind them all is Solstice Press, a small publishing company in the northern Rockies. I'm especially thankful for having worked with Ivar Nelson, who believed in the concept of the book so much that he skied with me for ten days across the Gospel-Hump Wilderness through some of the worst skiing conditions possible. I'm also grateful for the support of other members of that party, Sandy Gebhards, Jerry Dixon, Linda Burke, Jim Flannigan, Pete Casavina, Phil Schofield and Scott Findholt who were fine companions on an unforgettable journey.

I'd like to thank the many others who helped, including the Sawtooth Gang; Kris Williams, Buzz Cheatham and Mary Naylor, and the good folks at Busterback Ranch. Thanks also to the Targhee Ski Patrol, my typist Dana Meyers, and Jack Stephenson.

A special thanks to those who reviewed the manuscript and provided me with very helpful suggestions, including Bob Winslow, Idaho State University; Kirk Bachman, Leonard Expeditions; Bob Woodward, *Ski's Guide to Cross-Country Skiing*; and Rod Newcomb, American Avalanche Institute.

And, of course, to "H" Hilbert, who first turned me on to cross-country skiing, and whom I can never thank enough.

Contents

PLANNING

Backcountry trips on Nordic skis can be taken wherever there's snow and relatively wild land. These trips can be exhilarating runs through hardwood forests in the East, quiet ski trips through the open spaces of the plains, voyageur's trails in the boundary lakes of Ontario and Minnesota, or winter camping in nearby state or provincial parks. Chances are that there are areas in the backcountry near you that you never expected offered skiing opportunities because you have never been there in the winter.

There's fine skiing in such unexpected places as the Grand Canyon in Arizona, and among the rainbow terraces and spires of Bryce Canyon in southern Utah. You can ski at elevations up to 10,000 feet in New Mexico at the Valle Grande crater or in the Pecos Wilderness.

In Canada, there are splendid hut systems in the Laurentian Mountains in Quebec, and in the Rockies in British Columbia and Alberta. There's wilderness skiing from the Labrador Coast to Kluane National Park in the Yukon.

How to decide where to ski? I won't say. It can depend on where you live, how far you want to travel or how much time you have to get there and back. Part of the fun is in the choosing. You might have favorite areas close by where you've been on day trips but want to push further from the trailhead. A preferred hiking area in the summer could turn out to be fine touring in the winter. Whenever I'm out backpacking, I always look for prospective winter trips. More ideas for trips can come from friends, salesmen at your favorite cross-country speciality shop, clubs, magazines and guidebooks.

Skiing nearby is not a bad idea. Most of us are concerned about the environment and conserving resources. Reducing driving distances certainly helps. We often think good skiing is far away. There's good powder in the West, they say, and that's certainly true at times. But even though I live in a powder kingdom, I still use klisters as often as blue wax. The far West, East, and Midwest have their powder days too. They may be rare, but when those days come, they're really special. Develop an eye for what makes your region unique. Grand, open panoramas are found in the West; subtle beauty awaits the skier in the Midwest lake system; and the elegant scenery of thick forests beckons in the East.

The nice thing about winter is that it expands the summer backcountry. Roads that give easier access in the summer are closed by deep snow, and the backcountry becomes larger, further away, and more wild.

Some skiers enjoy one area, returning trip after trip, each time discovering something new. Some have only small pockets of wild areas for their backcountry skiing. The distances traveled on skis in these areas may be small, but skiers come to know the area in a more intimate way. Western skiers, for example, can easily think in terms of lots of mileage through wilderness. There's so much of it. But because of the acreage available, they may pass quickly through an area, missing interesting sights and slopes and the little pleasures that are so important.

When

More comfortable temperatures occur in late winter and spring. This is the best time if you're just getting started on winter trips. It gives you a chance to develop a personal repertoire of ways of keeping warm and of comfortably enjoying the winter.

Camping in the winter can be cold. It can be miserable, especially for the unini-tiated, on cold December and January days. If you have several of these cold trips at the outset, you're liable to be turned off and miss the special pleasures of ski camping. Taking those first trips when it's warmer will help you get your equipment together for earlier winter trips when the mercury drops.

Near the base of the Grand Teton.

Information

Once you've decided on an area, the next step involves gathering information. Some skiers collect all possible data: maps; guidebooks; information from friends, shop owners, and fellow club members. From this information, they can determine the difficulty of skiing, good places to camp, interesting climbs, information on huts or cabins that are available (yes, some backcountry skiers

don't mind a little more comfort now and then), and possible powder bowls or open slopes for downhill runs.

Others gather very little information. They may have a map and some suggestions from a friend, but that's all. Sometimes that's the only available information, but at other times a skier gathers sparse information by choice. A famous British mountaineer once said if he couldn't plan a mountaineering expedition to the Himalayas on the back of an envelope, it wasn't worth doing. In the same vein, this type of tourer enjoys the spirit of discovering new things and meeting challenges. Important to this approach is an acute understanding of the potential dangers and acceptance of the risks involved.

Someone with sound experience can afford to gather limited information but it's foolish for beginning backcountry skiers not to seek advice. There's plenty of challenge without creating more. Even an experienced skier should at least gather weather and snow pack information in order to be prepared for any avalanche danger. This is essential information that doesn't interfere with the thrill of the unexpected.

The best sources of information for your tour are the Geological Survey topographic maps of the area.

Length of Tour

Backcountry ski tours can take several different forms. The "loop tour" starts from the trailhead and returns via a different route. The "up and back tour" returns via the same trail. The "downhill tour" follows a route which is mostly downhill after starting at the top of a pass, or after taking a ski lift up to the top of a ski area. The "traverse tour" crosses a range of mountains by starting at one point and ending at another. The "mountain ascent" uses Nordic skis to approach and climb a peak.

When planning the number of miles your party can ski each day, you have to

allow for the different conditions that will effect this mileage.

- How steep are the slopes, and how much up and down is there?
- Is there heavy brush, open water or slush on lakes, avalanche debris, bare ground? Are there difficult stream crossings, glacial crevasses?
- Are the packs exceptionally heavy?
- How fast is your slowest or weakest member?
- Will the snow be wet, or deep powder, or solid crust?
- Is the weather expected to be stormy or clear?

All of the conditions outlined above should be considered in the planning process. If the snow conditions are good as in a firm, spring crust, a skier conceivably could cover 15 miles or more each day. Most folks plan somewhere in the 5-to-12-mile range. Skiers on multiday tours will be carrying heavy packs which slow down the pace considerably. Remember that weather and snow conditions can vary dramatically from one day to the next.

How much should you plan, then? It really varies. I've been on tours where it was an easy day to cover 10 to 15 miles, and on other tours when 3 miles was a long, long day.

Mail carriers in early western history were faced with similar problems. In Idaho, there was a mail route over which the mail carriers used skis to travel in the winter between the mining towns of Idaho City and Banner, a distance of approximately 30 miles. One fine spring day in 1880, James Moore and James Irwin skied the route in 7 hours and 45 minutes.

The pace was not always so breath taking. Jimmy Emerson left Idaho City with the Banner mail on a Monday early in March. A week later, worn out from an unsuccessful journey, he returned with the Banner mail undelivered. After struggling for days, he had only reached a point eight miles from town. He returned his mail to the post office and, as the town's newspaper put it, "threw up his position."

To keep from being as frustrated as Jimmy Emerson, allow flexibility in your plans. Be ready to camp earlier than planned. Bring extra food along in case the trip takes a little longer. Shorten the tour if you find two feet of wet, new snow.

Some public land management agencies request backcountry skiers to fill out forms showing where they will camp each night. Their premise is that nature is predictable and constant in the winter, which is pure malarkey. No matter what the management agencies think, planning for ski tours is planning to be flexible. Realizing this, you're off to a good start.

Contingencies   Rescue

While you are reviewing maps and gathering information, develop some contingency plans for unexpected problems that could occur. Adverse weather, an injury, avalanche terrain, and high winds could cause troubles. Have a few ideas in mind on how you can deal with the situation. Before the trip and during the tour locate alternate routes you can follow if avalanche dangers get high. Watch out for protected places in case a sudden storm overtakes your party, and for an easy way out if someone gets hurt. These are the alternatives you should keep in mind or even write down on your maps. If you have carefully thought out contingency plans, you will be better prepared if something does happen.

Some skiers feel that free or inexpensive rescue services should be provided by society and readily available to anyone who gets in trouble in the outdoors. Others are opposed to any form of rescue service, feeling that if a skier runs into trouble, it is his or her responsibility. Anyone who is in a dangerous situation would be grateful for rescue assistance. The problem is that some people develop a false sense of security and go into dangerous areas ill-prepared. This results in more rescues, and higher costs, which bring on more regulation, making the skiing experience more restricted, less free and less adventurous.

You should always strive to be as self-reliant as possible. Bring good equipment, which you know works. Have training in first aid. Use common sense, turn back if you have to. The backcountry will always be there for you to return to again.

Most problems you'll encounter will be minor and you'll be able to divide up the injured person's pack and help him or her ski out to safety. However, you should prepare beforehand for the possibility of more serious situations by:

- Letting friends know where you are going by giving them a map and approximate itinerary.
- Knowing in advance where the nearest helicopter service is located.
- For very serious situations, know in advance whom to call for assistance.

Groups

The best way to get started in back-country skiing is to go with a group. Members of the group can share their knowledge and skills with you. In some places, there are organized groups that take backcountry trips regularly. In other places, you'll find friends interested in backcountry skiing.

Four is a good size for a winter ski party. If someone is injured, one person can stay while the other two go for help. An ideal number, however, isn't always attainable. Many times, only two or three skiers can be found. Although most skiers don't let that stop them, they are aware of the added risks and take extra care.

Unless you go with a formal school or guide service, leadership will be largely on a democratic basis. Normally, the person with the most experience carries the weight when making decisions but all members can help in the process. In this way, the group is made stronger since the party can combine the resources of all members. Emergencies call for an appropriately knowledgeable person, such as a doctor in a medical emergency, to take over and direct the other members.

From the beginning, all members need to work for the good of the entire group and not for personal whims and preferences. On longer trips, you would want to have along trustworthy and reliable party members.

Permits and Weather

Children

Some areas require winter permits and you may have to stop at a land manager's office (or Forest Service Ranger's) before reaching the trailhead. This is a good time for you to find out about snow conditions, to solve route finding problems, and to seek other bits of helpful information. If avalanche hazards exist along your route, the most important information to determine is the history of the snow pack, general terrain, and the weather. From this information, you can form some opinions about the avalanche hazard. Some areas have an avalanche warning system which gives the relative degree of danger. Ed LaChapelle, one of the foremost researchers in avalanche science, once defined "low" avalanche danger: "There's not much avalanche hazard, but a determined idiot could get in trouble."

If there is no land management office, you can still get some ideas about the snow pack. Check around at the nearest town. Stop at a bar. Find when the last snowfall was, how much snow fell, and what the weather and temperature patterns have been that winter.

When camping with children, ski only short distances; one to two miles is probably enough. Start out with a backyard camping experience to break in the idea. Remember, those first experiences are extremely important and you want them to be positive. If you're careful and use common sense while on trips, you can provide invaluable experiences for a child.

The one piece of equipment which is ideal for children is the Balata, a strap-in type binding. The binding consists of a leather strap system that can accommodate any boot. That way, you won't have to buy special cross-country ski boots.

Going Alone

Fletcher Manley

"Never go alone" is a warning often found in books about winter trips. I don't think it's a hard and fast rule. There are some skiers who feel sufficiently comfortable with their skills and knowledge of the outdoors that they may elect to travel alone. Being alone in the winter wilderness is an intense and richly rewarding experience. It opens up a new realm of awareness, not the least of which is learning about one's self. But the solo skier, more than anyone, needs to face the fact that potential dangers are greatly magnified. If injured, he will find himself in a grave situation. He should never expect rescue. Accepting the ultimate realities can be both his exhilaration and his grief.

High up in the French Alps.

9

Being in Shape

If you are healthy and active, you do not need a rigorous training program before going backcountry skiing. Anyone who gets out and jogs, plays tennis regularly, or goes cross-country skiing at every opportunity, is in good enough shape to take part in backcountry trips.

If, however, you sit in an office all week and catch a little golf on the weekend, you'll want to think about more preparation. It is not necessary to be on level six of the Royal Canadian Air Force exercise program, but you're not going to have fun and enjoy the trip if you become tired a mile from the trailhead. In consideration of your companions, remember that an unfit skier becomes a liability to the group.

To get in shape, concentrate on cardio-respiratory exercises. Cross-country skiing regularly is the best preparation but often isn't possible because of where we live. Jogging is a natural and can be done anywhere. If you don't like to jog, try swimming, vigorous tennis, handball or basketball. The idea is to do it regularly, consistently, and far enough in advance that your body can gradually adjust. Crash, get-in-shape programs may work for younger folks, but someone older than the mid-20's should give it some time. Besides, keeping fit feels good and keeps you happy.

In preparation for longer journeys, most skiers will step up their routine physical activities that they do each day.

Last Minute Checks

Your equipment has been gathered. The food is bought and packaged, and the day to leave on your trip is near. Here's a few last minute steps you should take to get ready:

Ski Bottoms. A good many books and magazine articles recommend applying a glide wax on most of the ski surfaces except the approximately two-foot long kicker zone. This is too much glide wax for the backcountry, especially for fiberglass skis. Many backcountry skiers don't worry about glide waxes and kicker zones and apply their grip waxes to the full length of the ski.

Stoves and other equipment. Fire up your stove and make sure it is operating properly. Check your bindings for any loose screws. Sort through your other equipment for rips or damages from the last outing and repair them before you leave.

Pack. Skiers have different ways of arranging their packs. You probably have your own ideas from summer backpacking

experiences. The objective should be to keep the weight low in the pack and next to your body to give stability on skis. Place heavier items in the lower portion of the pack and nearest your back. For long trips, you may have to lash some items such as a foam pad or a shovel to the outside of your pack. Try to lash them in such a way that it takes a minimum effort to strap them on and to take them off, and so that they don't wobble to and fro as you ski.

Notify a friend. Before leaving, let a friend know where you're going and when you expect to return. It's not a bad idea to give this friend a map of your route. Be sure to give yourself extra time. Bad weather and snow conditions can slow you down.

Weather forecast. If a major storm system is expected, some may decide to wait for another time to do the trip. Others welcome bad weather, but they should keep safe, protected, alternate routes in mind if avalanche danger increases because of heavy snow falls.

Vehicle. Make sure your vehicle is in good shape for winter driving. Antifreeze should be at full strength. Bring shovel and chains. Take jumper cables and tow rope for an emergency. In some places, it is difficult or risky to leave your vehicle at the trail head. Arrange well in advance for a shuttle to take it somewhere convenient and/or safe.

On the Road

Skiers get to their destination in numerous ways. They cram into a little Volkswagen among packs and sleeping bags and wearing down jackets because the heater doesn't work. Or they travel in luxury in a four-wheel drive vehicle with plenty of room to stretch legs and with stereo music. Sometimes skiers hitchhike, hoping that someone will pick them up even with their bulky packs and skis. Others fly in a small aircraft to remote areas. Whatever mode of transportation, it's a time to leave behind hassles and problems and to feel the anticipation and excitement of a winter adventure.

EQUIPMENT

In the old days, skis were quite simple: a straight, solid piece of wood with a steamed, up-turned tip. The boots were attached by a leather strap nailed to the ski, or slipped back through a slot cut in the ski. Some old-timers could make a pair in no time with a draw knife and a saw. Others were more meticulous and were known in their respective communities as ski craftsmen. One ski craftsman in Michigan could look at the shape of a tree and make a ski with natural camber.

Ski equipment manufacturers have come a long way since those days. Some feel that they have gone too far and created a lot of unnecessary equipment. But modern equipment allows us to go further into the backcountry and the right equipment can save us from the frustrations and hardships which plagued the old-timers. For those of you who might be hesitant to venture into the backcountry overnight for fear of not having the right equipment, take heart. There are many choices in helpful equipment.

In fact, the choices can be overwhelming if you don't know what you are looking for, especially for those prone to bring the proverbial kitchen sink. Being under- or overequipped can be a problem. This section will help you to make the choices, offer hints on what features to look for, and help you judge the carrying capacity of backcountry skiing equipment. It will also help in deciding how much to invest in equipment and give tips about improvising. One of the interesting aspects of ski camping is the way it encourages skiers to suit their own needs and styles.

Skis

Wood skis have been around for a long time. But more backcountry skiers are switching—some reluctantly—to fiberglass. Good fiberglass skis will be as much as ten times the strength of a good hickory ski. Fiberglass skis can be more carefully controlled during construction to give them different flex and camber patterns. Wood skis, however, handle well in powder conditions. They climb very well, while fiberglass users are slipping and changing to a softer wax. In some spring conditions, the pine tar base of wood skis can be stripped off by the coarse snow, causing the ski to pick up moisture, preventing glide altogether. Though fiberglass skis offer a distinct edge over wood skis, a few skiers hang on to their traditional wood skis. There's something that feels good and is aesthetically pleasing about them. What a pleasure it is to ski the powder on a pair of finely made wooden boards.

Ski Characteristics. Skis are classified by their width at the *waist* near the mid-point of the ski in the binding area. Here's a chart for quick reference during the following discussion of skis:

Basic Types of Skis Classified by Width at the Waist

Racing	42 to 48 mm
Light Touring	46 to 52 mm
Touring	52 to 61 mm
Mountaineering	55 mm and over

The above measurements of the ski are taken at the waist, but just as important to the backcountry skier is the measurement of the *tip* or *shovel* of the ski. Backcountry skis usually will have a wider shovel than waist. This gives the ski a curve along its sides which is known as *side camber*.

Side camber helps the ski turn when edged on downhill runs. Some manufacturers, however, disagree and say cross-country skiers never ski fast enough to where side camber is important. They say that it is actually the ski bowing by the skier's weight that helps to make the turn. My experience is that side cut is definitely an asset for the backcountry skier. Try a ski with and without side cut on a packed snow surface. The difference will be apparent.

What are the best combinations of side camber and width in skis? It depends with whom you talk. Ned Gillete, well known for his ski expeditions around Mt. McKinley and across Ellesmere Island, has used skis with a 47 mm waist and a 55 mm shovel. Ed Baldwin, cross-country ski writer, competitor and telemark expert from the steep hardwood forests of the East, recommends a ski waist width of 60 mm with a shovel of 70 to 85 mm.

Comparing these preferences shows how much of a leeway there is in choosing the width of skis. If you own only a pair of light touring skis, you can get along on backcountry trips. But if backcountry skiing is your love or if you are in the market for a ski specifically for back-country skiing, your best bet is a width somewhere between the Gillette-Baldwin extremes. Waist width in the mid-50 mm range and above combined with a shovel that is 10 mm wider than the waist will provide the best all-around ski.

Camber, the arch of the skis, should also be considered when buying skis. Beware of the rigamarole over double cambered skis. Double cambered skis are stiffly arched and require a vigorous kick to weight the entire ski against the snow. That may be great for a racer, but it's pure hell for the backcountry skier. No backcountry skier will be vigorously kicking and gliding with a pack on his back full of camping gear, clothing, and food. If anything, camber should be soft, not as soft as a wet noodle, but soft enough for the ski to be easily flattened by the skier's weight. Fiberglass skis have particularly

fast bases and a ski that's even a little too soft won't drag noticeably. A soft ski also helps considerably when you're climbing and depending on a good grip.

In addition to camber, skis flex differently from the tip area through the midsection to the tail. Different areas of the ski have different degrees of flexibility. This is a little more difficult to determine. You can get a feel for it by flexing different skis while you're in specialty shops. To flex the tip, grab the waist and pull the tip toward you. Feel how stiff the tip is and watch how the ski bows as you pull the tip back. A good backcountry ski has a soft tip. To flex the tail, hold the ski firmly and

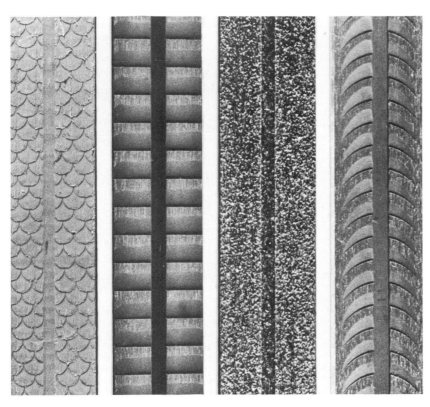

Waxless ski bottoms:
from left - *fishscale,*
step, mica and radial
step.

push the tail into the floor so the tail bends. A good ski will have a stiffer tail than tip. Try different skis and compare.

The standard method of measuring length by standing with your hand above your head works fine for backcountry skis. If the tip comes to the wrist of your extended arm, the length is correct. Some skiers will drop down some centimeters in length to give them better handling.

Wood skis are made in laminations for strength and flex characteristics. Fiberglass skis are made by a number of different glassing techniques. No matter what particular process is used, reputable ski manufacturers will produce strong skis. Many of the manufacturers offer one- or two-year breakage guarantees.

Unfortunately, there is a lot of junk on the market. Some manufacturers saw they could make money on the cross-country ski market by throwing together fiberglass skis. One of your best protections is to buy from a cross-country speciality shop. Even then ski technology is progressing so fast with manufacturers trying so many new processes that shop salespersons can be confused. Remember the basics and what to look for. Use caution in considering new materials that haven't been field tested. Ask the salesperson if he or she has tried it under a variety of conditions. Check with others who have used the product and check equipment reviews in outdoor magazines. Conservative buying will pay off in the long run.

Waxless skis. Whether to use wax or waxless skis can produce a difference of opinion among cross-country skiers. Most cross-country ski authorities now agree that a wax ski can outperform a waxless ski on a track. Little, however, has been said of the use of waxless skis in the backcountry where minimizing the hassles that come with waxing skis can be a big advantage.

I've always been a wax ski advocate myself. Recently, though, I was on a long ski trek and encountered a variety of

conditions from soft, deep powder, to transitional snow, to coarse, spring snow, to icy, avalanche rubble. One member of our party used a pair of fishscale skis. Many times I watched in amazement from the side of the trail with my waxes spread out while Sandy skied by. Her skis were more than adequate for the great variety of snow conditions we encountered.

Waxless skis are criticized on the basis of glide which, while important for track skiing, is not as important for backcountry skiing. The ski shouldn't be so slow that you work to push it forward. Good grip, characteristic of many waxless skis, is desirable with a pack on your back when little slips cause face forward falls in the snow. Another convenience of the waxless ski is that you don't need the extra weight and space of a wax kit (with the possible exception of glider wax) and it saves time, especially in difficult conditions, spent waxing skis. If you haven't tried waxless, you might want to ski on a few pairs. Borrow a pair from a friend or rental shop. Saving weight, time, and hassles is something that is welcomed in the backcountry.

Boots

This discussion will center on ski touring boots, but it is entirely possible to use regular hiking boots with a cable binding. On a 175-mile journey I took in 1973, we used hiking boots and cable bindings. They worked well although cable bindings can be hard on hiking boots. Rubber pack boots can be used with cables as well as old leather Alpine ski boots that have had the midsole removed. Heavy cross-country ski boots are commonly used with cables. If you use cable bindings and have had problems with breakage, try *ABC*

Victory bindings. They're one of the better bindings for rugged use.

Pin bindings are comfortable and flexible. With a sturdy, rigid boot, they give you the same or better control than cables. Pin binding boots for backcountry range from the lighter models to heavy duty boots with *Vibram* soles. A back-country skier wants a sturdy boot that will keep feet warm. The boot should be sturdy enough to walk on bare ground or across wind-swept areas. Most of these types of boots fall in the regular three-pin binding (Nordic Norm) category where the width of binding at the pins is either 71, 75, or 79 mm. A smaller binding (New Nordic Norm) is 50 mm across at the binding and is being used by some backcountry skiers. Adidas has a 38 mm boot and Dynafit has brought out the Lin boot system.

Here are some considerations when buying a pair of boots for backcountry:

Warmth. Cold feet are no fun. Make sure the boot has at least the thickness of a hiking boot. While leather is now the best material, changes are bound to come.

Cable binding.

Bindings

Of all equipment, boots are the furthest behind in development. Warmth of a boot can be increased by adding inserts, but don't make the boot too tight. Various types of overboots are available which slip over the boot and help keep feet toasty. Warmth also can be increased by slipping an old sock over the boot. It's amazing how much extra warmth can be gained by the old sock trick. Try it when it's cold and notice the difference.

Torsional Rigidity. Hold a boot by its toe and heel, and twist. A good backcountry boot should twist with a lot of resistance, or not twist at all. If a boot twists easily, it will be more difficult for you to control your skis down hills.

Forward Flex. Because of its rigidity, a backcountry boot won't flex forward as easily as a regular touring boot. A little stiffness doesn't hurt when making kick turns, side-stepping in powder, or trying to break through soggy snow in the spring.

Materials. Leather is the best bet. Stitched soles now have a better reputation than molded soles. Fleece liners can become wet and present drying problems, but so do leather ones.

Comfort. Your boot should fit like hiking boots. Make sure you have room to curl your toes. When the boot flexes, it shouldn't bind your toes. When you fit a boot, bring your socks along. The boot shouldn't be tight fitting. Tight boots are a major cause of cold feet.

Nordic Norm pin bindings come in three sizes: 71, 75, and 79 mm. The 71 mm size is for very small boots. On some larger boots, especially those with *Vibram* soles, you'll want to make sure your binding is large enough for the boots. Nothing is more frustrating than spending five minutes trying to get your boot into a tight binding. It is best to go with a 79 mm binding for larger boots and to use a hammer to tap in its sides so that the boot fits.

Bindings have different types of bails for clamping down the toe. For backcountry use, you'll want to have a strong bail. I have seen wire bails break on ski trips. Plate bails are definitely stronger and they exert a more even pressure on the protruding sole of the boot than wire bails. Bails can pop out and break so it's a good idea to carry extras along.

Poles

At the turn of the century, a single "balancing" pole was used. It was placed between the legs as a brake to slow a skier when descending a steep slope. Good skiers could make turns back and forth using the pole as a rudder. At times, the balancing pole, as its name implies, served the same purpose as a tightrope walker's pole and was held horizontally for balancing on downhill runs. It also helped to propel the skier along the flat. And, in a survival situation, an occasional half-crazed old-timer used his pole as a club to chase wild game.

Two poles have now replaced one, but the old techniques are still in use. The between-the-leg technique has gotten me safely down some icy trails. Although I've never had to use my poles as clubs to chase game, one of these days they might come in handy to use on a snowmobile.

As with fiberglass for skis, synthetic materials are replacing natural cane for poles. Fiberglass poles work well for backcountry. Aluminum, because of its strength, has been another favorite.

Most backcountry skiers are satisfied with the usual round basket. The common size is around 11 to 12 mm (4½" to 4¾") in diameter. Larger baskets are available for powder snow.

Many poles have plastic grips. The older, rough leather grips were nice since they weren't quite as slippery. Adjustable straps on the poles are a must. On a warm day, you may ski with liners while on a cold day you may wear a bulky pair of mittens. The straps should be large enough to accommodate your thickest mittens.

Pole length for backcountry skiing is measured the same way as for normal touring. The pole should fit into the armpit.

Ski Accessories

Heel Popper. Good heel poppers have sharp, serrated edges which help keep the heel of the boot in place when going downhill. The main function of the heel popper is as an aid in knocking snow off heels of boots. It doesn't always work, but it helps.

Heel Locators. The function of a heel locator is to hold the heel of the boot, giving you more control. There are various types of heel locators on the market. Some are wedge-shaped and fit into a notch in the heel of the boot. The idea is good, but in practice the heel slips off too easily. The *Loipus* heel locator has a plastic post that is screwed into the heel of the boot which slides into an elongated "V" shaped plastic assembly mounted on the ski. This is a more effective means of holding the heel of the boot in place for downhill without sacrificing any of the mobility of the pin bindings. While heel locators help, they will not make anyone an instant mountaineering downhill skier. The *Loipus* locators are often mounted in reverse and facing backwards. Other effective types of heel locators are appearing on the market.

Skins and climbers. Skins and rope climbers are put on the bottom of skis to help climb steep slopes. Both provide a rough surface on the bottom of the ski

Loipus heel locators.

which will grip the snow in situations where the ski would otherwise slip.

Skins consist of a cloth base with small hairs all oriented in the same direction. They are particularly useful in rugged terrain with a lot of ups and downs. They provide superb climbing ability on steep pitches, and can be left on to slow a skier on downhill runs that otherwise would be too fast. The adhesive-backed skins which stick to the bottom of the ski don't allow snow to build up under the skin as easily as the skins that strap on.

Rope climbers are made with ¼" polypropylene rope woven around the ski and tied with figure eight knots under the ski and overhand knots on top of the ski. They can be easily made, or purchased commercially. Rope climbers work well when climbing in soft snow conditions but are a little slippery on hard crust. They are also useful when travelling in very brushy areas as they turn the ski into a snowshoe and give the skier more maneuverability. I also use rope climbers when descending steep, icy trails.

Rope climbers.

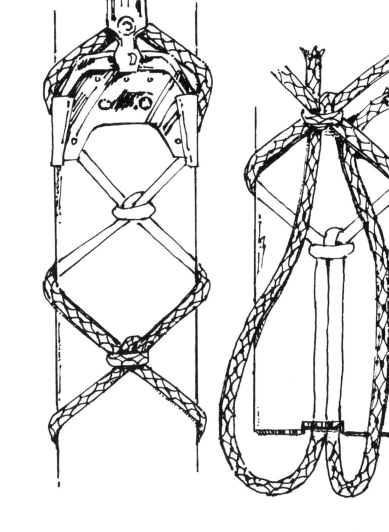

25

Packs

There are three types of packs for overnight journeys:

External frame pack. This is the classic backpack with an external (usually aluminum) frame. It is efficient for handling heavy loads, and is used by many backcountry skiers. There are disadvantages. This pack is very unwieldy for skiing, having a distinct sideways wobble which can occur at the most inopportune times. It restricts poling and prevents extension of the arms. The top aluminum braces can bang a skier in the back of the head during a fall. Despite the disadvantages, many skiers already have a frame pack from their summertime backpacking and don't want the extra expense of buying a new pack. Others just don't feel comfortable with a heavily loaded soft or internal frame pack.

Soft pack. This type of pack utilizes no frame at all. The *Jensen* pack is an example and it is one of the first which became popular for ski touring. It has, however, a limited weight capacity.

Internal frame pack. The most popular pack with backcountry skiers is designed to conform to your back. It bends and twists with you, giving a greater degree of balance. The hip suspension systems on internal frame packs have been improved to the point that many packs now on the market carry loads on the hips quite comfortably. Most of the good internal frame packs are adjustable to different skier's heights and body frames. Some have aluminum stays which can be bent to conform to your back.

Packs—from left to right: internal frame, day pack, cat, external frame.

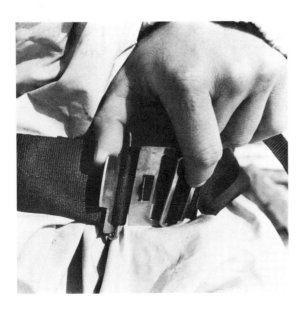

Here are some additional features to consider when in the market for a pack:

Size. Packs are measured in cubic inches. It is better to buy a large capacity pack that will carry all your winter equipment. If you're using fiberfill jackets and sleeping bags, a larger capacity pack is necessary for the bulkiness. I like a large pack since I'm a poor packer. When it's cold in the morning, I don't want to take the time to make sure all my stuff bags are neatly packed. I throw things in the pack as quickly as possible and get moving. A large pack helps me do this. The volume range to consider is four thousand cubic inches or larger.

Hip suspension. It's important to have a good hip suspension system on a pack. Carrying the load on your waist makes all the difference in the world. As you ski along, you can adjust the weight between waist and shoulders.

Front loading and top loading. Front loading packs zip open and expose the entire front of the pack while top loaders are the traditional type in which items are stuffed in from the top. All the contents are easily accessible in a front loading pack, but, beware, zippers can break and cause problems. Some like top loading packs because they can keep piling things in, then top it off with a sleeping pad and strap it down which gives them a little more capacity.

Adjustment straps. Straps should be easily adjustable while you're skiing. You should be able to draw the load close to your back or let it out, and to adjust the hip belt and shoulder straps without taking the pack off. Packs should be adjustable to fit your body frame. A salesman at a speciality shop can help.

Fit. You never know how a pack feels until it has weight in it. While trying on packs at a store, put in a sleeping bag, down jacket, stove, wool shirt, and other odds and ends around the shop. Load the pack as you would if you were going on a ski trip. If the store is a good one, they'll let you do it because they realize how important it is to fit packs with a load. Walk around the store. Swing your arms, bend over, and kneel down. Make a mental note of how it feels and compare it to others. Different packs will feel different to different people.

Stitching. Eight to ten stitches per inch is best. Check stress areas to make sure they are reinforced.

Buckles. What type of buckle should you have on the waist belt? Quick release buckles are a real asset when you are crossing streams, avalanche slopes, or falling face first in the snow. If the pack doesn't have a quick release buckle, you can purchase one at a speciality shop. *Kelty* makes a good waist buckle.

Compression straps. Compression straps are built into the sides of some packs so that the pack can be pulled in to compress the contents. They are particularly useful to bring a light load in close to the back. They are handy but not absolutely necessary.

Carrying skis. There always will be times when you will have to walk and carry your skis: crossing avalanche rubble, dry spots, windswept areas, and streams. Packs which have some type of arrangement, such as compression straps, sleeves, or special pockets for carying skis are a definite asset at such times.

Side pockets. Side pockets are handy for storing smaller items. They can, however, get in the way and restrict the swing of your arms. On my *Lowe* pack, I sewed a few extra tabs on the rear of the pack so the side pockets are still attached to the side but further to the rear where they don't restrict arm motion quite so much. Many skiers don't worry too much about their arm swing and side pockets aren't a problem to them.

Accessories. Other items that go along with a pack include straps for lashing on equipment. If you will be in an area where rain is a strong possibility, you might want to bring along a waterproof pack covering. Pack covers are available on the market, or you can adapt a tarp or bivouac bag with a little *Velcro*. Even if a pack is made from waterproof material it won't be completely waterproof. The many seams on a pack are all potential leaks. A waterproof pack covering prevents this and assures that everything inside the pack will be dry.

Sleeping Bags

The most commonly used sleeping bags for backcountry skiing have two types of insulating fills: synthetic fiberfills and down. Down is still the lightest, the least bulky, and if taken care of, lasts longer. But down picks up body moisture quickly and will gradually lose loft on a winter ski trip. I've watched my down bag wilt to a couple of pieces of nylon over a several day trip. Down isn't a good choice for winter use unless you're only out a couple of days or if you use a vapor barrier.

Vapor barriers in sleeping bags are becoming more popular. Some sleeping bags are constructed with waterproof interiors. A breathable bag can be converted by using a waterproof inner bag. It is best to buy or make this inner bag with a lengthwise zipper so that the bag can be easily ventilated. The sleeping bag is then protected from loft-reducing body moisture. To add even more protection to the system, a waterproof bivouac sack can be pulled over sleeping bag to help prevent frost or other outside moisture from wetting the bag. The vapor barrier and waterproof bivouac bag forms a fairly watertight system which can make down much more practical for winter use.

There are other sleeping bag combinations. Some bags are made with a down top and fiberfill bottom. *Camp Seven* makes a fiberfill overbag that you can pull over your summer down or fiberfill bag to increase its warmth for winter camping. That's not a bad idea since it is a versatile system and uses the layer principle which is so important in the winter. For several years, I successfully used a fiberfill bag and a down, half bag inside. The down, half bag was the type that can be converted to down pants in very cold conditions.

Bivouac bags (bivy sacks) are used by many winter campers to protect the outside of the bag from moisture. It also adds another layer and some warmth to the bag. However, unless winter temperatures are warm, a bivouac bag can have problems. The body moisture that passes through the sleeping bag hits the cooler nylon layer of the bivouac bag and will condense as moisture and frost between the bivouac bag and the sleeping bag. This moisture can get into the insulation of your sleeping bag and destroy some of its insulating qualities.

Phil Schofield, who did most of the photography for this book, was on a 10-day ski trip with me. He used a *Gore-Tex* bivouac sack and woke every morning with a down bag which was wetter and losing more loft each day. Finally, on the last morning, he announced he had learned the secret of a *Gore-Tex* bivouac bag: Don't sleep in it; sleep on top of it.

If you're in the market for a sleeping bag, here are some additional considerations:

Loft. Most sleeping bag manufacturers will rate their bags to certain temperature ranges. These ratings are not of too much value to the skier since there is no industrial standard to compare ratings. Besides, individuals vary in their needs. What might be comfortable for one person at 0 degrees F, might be an icebox for another. The best way to compare bags is by their loft. You can measure loft yourself by bringing a ruler with you to the speciality shop. To measure loft, put the sleeping bag into its stuff bag, wait a few minutes, then pull it out. Shake it a few times, then measure in the chest area from the floor to the top of the bag. For an approximate rating of comfort, five to six inches of total loft (top to bottom) will be good down to 20 degrees F. Eight inches of loft will be good down to 0 degrees F. Many skiers buy a 20 degree F bag and plan to wear clothing to improve its comfort range. A cold sleeper may want to go with the 0 degree F bag.

Shape. The mummy-shaped bag is the most efficient for winter sleeping. Be sure you have enough room to wear your winter clothing inside the bag. When shopping for a bag, slip on a down or fiberfill jacket and climb into the bag. If the bag is tight then the loft and relative warmth of the bag will be reduced.

Length. Buy a bag long enough so that your feet do not press against the end when you are inside the bag. Some skiers will buy a bag a size longer so they will have room to put their boots into the bottom of the bag.

Hood. The head and neck are the important heat loss areas of the body. A hood on a sleeping bag is a must. You should be able to draw the hood up to a small hole for breathing. Some sleeping bags have a down collar that fits around the neck and adds even more insulation.

Other features. A full-length zipper is vital for ventilation on warmer nights. Check the stitching; 8 to 10 stitches

per inch is ideal. Check for reinforced areas at stress points.

Here are a few things you can do to keep your sleeping bag in tiptop shape:

- Keep sleeping bag fluffed and out of its stuff bag when storing between trips. Hang the bag in a closet. If space is a problem, put it in a huge stuff bag. You can easily make one out of an old sheet.

- Try to avoid washing a down bag. I've known some who have never washed their bag. I'm glad they keep it well aired out. When the moment of truth finally comes, you can either send it out or do it yourself. If you have a dry cleaner do the work, make sure they use a gentle cleaner like *Stoddard* fluid.

If you wash it by hand, use one of the down soaps (available at speciality shops), or *Ivory Flakes*. Wash it in your bathtub and treat it like a baby. Carry it gently to a drier and dry it on low heat with a couple of tennis balls thrown in to help the loft.

- Be sure *not* to send a fiberfill bag to a dry cleaner. The fluids will ruin it. Contrary to down bags, a fiberfill bag can be cleaned more often. Wash it in a bathtub, wring it out, and let it drip dry.

Sleeping Pads   Tents

A sleeping pad will help to keep you warm at night. There are two basic types—open cell and closed cell.

The effectiveness of closed-cell pad insulation is a factor to be considered by winter campers. Some of the polyethylene and ethylene-vinyl-acetate pads do not crack except at extremely low temperatures which won't be encountered even in high-elevation climbing trips to Alaska. I've used a pad called *Regalite* and sold by *Sierra West* that has worked splendidly. The pad is bulkier and a little harder to roll, so it is usually the last item under the top flap of the pack. It is surprisingly light.

How thick a pad should you use? An open cell pad should be at least two inches thick since it will compress substantially when you sleep on it. A closed-cell pad, which compresses very little, should be one-half to one inch thick. I prefer an even thicker pad. I use a full length, one-half inch pad on which I have glued two more one-half inch pads for the area under my back. Other skiers don't glue their pads together and are able to use them for other purposes such as cooking or standing on. When I've been cold on trips, I've felt it first from the ground. With this thickness, the effective range of my sleeping bag is greatly increased. On one trip, I used an old fiberfill bag with only four inches of total loft and wore only long johns, yet I was comfortable in temperatures around 15° F.

Tents come in a multitude of colors and shapes. Basic shapes include pyramid, tunnel, dome, and A-frame with a myriad of in between styles and forms. The most efficient use of space is in the tunnel and dome tents. However, if your location gets heavy, intensive, and wet snowfalls, you will have to be careful not to allow the snow to build up on the dome tent and collapse it. Pyramid tents are the easiest to set up. Stake down four corners, put the center pole inside, and voilà, home is ready. The center pole makes a convenient post on which to tie a candle for reading, cooking, or sorting out gear. A-frame tents are good in high winds, but they always feel cramped, and the tent walls invariably hang in your face.

One important consideration when buying a tent is how easily it can be set up while wearing mittens. The mitten test is something you should give all your winter equipment. When it's cold, the last thing you'll need is to have to pull off your mittens, grab a cold aluminum pole, and try to push it through a tight nylon sleeve, which is a hard task even in summer weather.

No matter how breathable or how well vented a tent might be, when it's cold the tent will collect frost on the inside walls during the night. Some tents have "frost liners" for this problem, but they are actually more hassle and extra weight than they're worth.

Many skiers don't worry about tent stakes. For them, skis and poles work fine. Others bring along a few sand and snow stakes which work well in the winter and are nice to have if you like to catch a little skiing after your tent is up. Some just use sticks tied to tent cords and buried in the snow.

Color of tents is important. Choose tent colors that are pleasing. When my business partner, Ike Gayfield, and I started our mountain shop known as Mountain Folk, we manufactured tents. Ike, who has a knack for form and aesthetics in outdoor equipment, designed a tent with pleasing yellow nylon that was always cheery inside even on gray days. We used the tents extensively in the winter, and they worked superbly. But we had been lax about testing our waterproof version in the rain. Before we had a chance to test it, we were besieged by requests for the tent. On one trip, several of my friends were in Mountain Folk tents. It poured throughout the night. I was cosy and dry in a Mountain Folk tarp. But as I walked around that morning, I found gloomy, tight-lipped friends curled around puddles of water in soggy sleeping bags. Soon after, Mountain Folk went out of the manufacturing business and concentrated on retailing.

Stoves

A good stove is necessary in winter. During stormy weather and cold mornings, you can cook right in the tent for convenience or just outside the door while remaining in the sleeping bag. Meals can be cooked quickly without having to wait around a fire, and water can be easily heated to warm you up. Stoves are essential in emergencies when you need hot liquids to ward off hypothermia.

Small, self-pressurizing stoves, such as the *Svea 123* with the *Sigg* cook kit, work satisfactorily in the winter, but the most reliable are the larger, heat-output stoves like the *Optimus 111-B, Phoebus 625,* and the *Mountain Safety Research*

Stoves—from left to right: Optimus 111B, Mountain Safety Research, Svea 123.

[MSR] stove. The *111-B* has proven itself in many ski and mountaineering expeditions, but it weighs three pounds, six ounces. The lighter, 12-ounce *MSR* stove uses a *Sigg* fuel bottle as a gas tank, saving the weight of a built-in gas tank. Because of its light weight and good heat output, many winter campers are using it. The base of the *MSR* is a little tipsy and you have to be careful that large pots don't fall off.

There are also cartridge stoves which use a butane or propane cartridge. When the gas supply is exhausted, you simply screw on a new cartridge. Most of these stoves don't work well in cold temperatures and the throwaway cartridges are a waste of resources.

The *111-B, MSR,* and *Phoebus* stoves use white gas (*Coleman* or *Blazo* fuels are advised). The fuel is extremely flammable. When possible, cook outside the tent. Other safety reminders are explained in the chapter titled *Camping and Cooking.* To reduce danger, use solid fuel pellets for priming the stove. These are available at hardware and sporting goods stores.

Fuel bottles are another necessary item. The round, aluminum *Sigg* bottles are common and reliable. Square bottles occasionally split along welded seams. When you buy bottles, make sure the lid has a gasket to prevent leakage. A useful feature found on some fuel bottles is a small hole in the cap. When the cap is partially unscrewed, fuel can be poured from the small opening. This is particularly handy when sprinkling fuel on the bottom of the ski to remove klister.

A funnel is needed to pour gas into stove fuel tanks. Some funnels available in speciality shops come with a little screen to keep out impurities.

For cooking, you'll need pots. Two pots are plenty for a group of four. Pot grippers are useful for removing hot pots from the stove but if you carry a small vice grip or pliers in your repair kit, that will work just as well. A two or four-cup plastic cup and a spoon are all you need for eating utensils. Any extra utensils, other than your pocket knife, are extra weight.

Repair kit  Emergency kit

A repair kit is essential and should contain enough repair items to fix any breakage or damage that might occur. A *sewing needle,* or sewing awl, and nylon thread, or dental floss, will take care of ripped clothing. *Duct tape,* or strapping tape, is very versatile and will repair a multitude of things from putting ski poles back together to putting a temporary patch on torn nylon. A good place to carry tape is wrapped around the ski pole to form a knob just below the handle. The tape is readily available, and forms a good grip for skiing on side hills. Some skiers carry a piece of *sheet metal* about five to six inches long and two to three inches wide for broken poles. It makes a sturdier splint than using broken sticks. *Epoxy* can be used to replace screws which have been torn out or to fix delaminated skis. Epoxy repairs should be done near a heat source for the resin and hardener to work properly.

Bring *extra screws* to fit your bindings. Many screws used now are posi-drive screws and not Phillips. Be sure to bring along a special posi-drive screwdriver if you do have these screws. The *vice-grips* have a multitude of uses (pot grippers, clamp for gluing delaminated skis, wire cutters) and they replace the less useful pliers. Other repair items include an *extra ski tip, clevis pins* (if you use an external frame backpack), *extra baskets, extra bails* to fit your bindings, some *bailing wire,* and *cables* for cable binding users.

Matches are one of the most important items to carry. Keep matches in several different places: in your stove, hidden in stuff bags, and in a waterproof container in your pocket. Along with the matches, carry fire starter (such as solid fuel pellets), compass, and knife in your pocket in case you get separated from your group and your pack. In your pack, you may also want to have a small stuff bag that contains more fire starter, matches, and perhaps a whistle.

Broken ski pole, duct tape and sheet metal sleeve.

Wax kit

You should keep your waxes to a minimum on a backcountry tour. In addition to a cork and scraper, some skiers simply carry the two-wax system and leave it at that.

One March, I was on a 50-mile trip to view a falls. The morning skiing was on blue klister, late morning on purple, and afternoon on red klister. It seemed I was always putting on and taking off wax. One of the skiers in the party let me try *Jack Rabbit* wet and it worked fine for all three conditions. *Swix Starter, Rex,* and *Toko* work well on fiberglass skis. Some skiers bring a more extensive wax kit. On my last three-week trip, I carried paraffin (from a candle), binder wax, green, extra blue, purple, *Jack Rabbit* wet, and blue, red, and yellow klisters. The addition of a small rag in your stuff bag is a great asset for cleaning skis. Keep the klisters, which are notorious for breaking open and leaving a sticky mess in stuff bags and packs, contained in separate ziplock plastic bags.

Ski pole repaired on the trail.

Other items

A *first aid kit* is important and a suggested list of contents is presented at the end of this chapter. *Sunglasses* or sun protection is a must. Some skiers carry two pairs. Gray-colored glasses are the best for visual clarity. Yellow glasses don't screen out enough ultraviolet in bright sunlight but are very helpful in flat light conditions. There are some glasses that turn different colors depending on light conditions—yellow in flat light and gray in bright sunlight.

A *headlamp* is an invaluable asset. I like to carry the four-battery type and use it extensively. Other smaller headlights are also available. Alkaline batteries last longer and work better in cold weather than regular carbon batteries. Any battery will work more efficiently when it's warm, and I always carry my battery pack in my pocket. There are expensive lithium batteries available from such sources as *Mountain Safety Research* in Seattle that outperform and outlast any other battery.

A *shovel* is another essential item. It can be used for digging snow caves, making tent platforms, digging a kitchen, and rescuing avalanche victims. Carry two in avalanche terrain, including one that is sturdy. The *Atlas*, size #2, grain scoop found at hardware and farming stores is a good one. *Snow saws* are very handy and can be used to make snow trenches and igloos.

If you are traveling in avalanche terrain, you should have either an electronic *beacon* or an *avalanche cord*. Poles which screw together into avalanche probes are also an important consideration. Even if you use electronic beacons to locate trapped victims, the avalanche probe is useful for a quick check of a buried person's location and is very handy in case the beacon stops working.

Avalanche probes can be used to check if the snow is deep enough for a snow cave. You can scratch scales of inches on the poles and use them for determining snow depth.

Nylon toggles are the best fasteners for winter use.

Some skiers carry *handwarmers* that use lighter fluid. Be sure there is ventilation since they give off fumes that could be deadly in closed areas.

Continually keep in mind as you acquire winter equipment whether that piece of equipment can be used while wearing mittens. One of the simplest and handiest particulars is a nylon cord attached to zippers on clothing, packs, and tents. The nylon cord makes it easy to use the zipper without removing mittens.

The best way to organize your pack is to use the stuff bag system where everything is put in differently colored stuff bags. Some even write with a magic marker on the stuff bag to indicate the contents. Toggles on stuff bags are very helpful. They save the time it takes to tie drawstrings and can be used with mittens.

Making
Your Own

The way the price of outdoor equipment is spiraling, making your own equipment is becoming more attractive. There are books available at bookshops and speciality stores which can help you get started. Another way of starting is to buy a kit. You'll be able to learn about seams, patterns, and sewing. Making your own kit teaches you about quality, which in turn makes you a more aware buyer.

Unless you are able to pick up bargains on sale at mountain shops, kits are less costly than buying retail. However, some of the less expensive kits, like vests, may not be cost efficient, especially if you've just started sewing. Once you get the hang of sewing, you'll come out ahead on such higher-priced equipment as tents and sleeping bags.

Some items are easy to make. Tarps, bivouac bags, vapor liners for sleeping bags, and stuff bags can be made very easily without having to buy a kit. More speciality shops are stocking basic raw materials.

Much of your backcountry equipment and present ski equipment can be used for backcountry skiing. It's not necessary to go out and buy all new equipment for winter camping. Make sure you have enough equipment to keep you warm. Check it out on a short, overnight trip and find out what works and what needs to be replaced. The idea is to get out there and enjoy the winter. With a little imagination, and borrowing an item or two, you can.

Equipment Lists

No matter how experienced the skier, he or she will go through an equipment list before each trip to be certain that everything is packed which is needed. Here are some suggested lists. We have provided check-off boxes before each item and suggest that you xerox the list before each tour and use it as a final check. More items are listed than you will actually bring in order to give you an idea of some of the different types of equipment that are possible for trips.

Some of the items can be shared. The tent and stove can be split up among the party. Repair and first aid kits can also be shared.

Clothing - Inner Layer

☐ Long john top and bottoms (wool or synthetic)
☐ Inner socks (wool or synthetic)
☐ Liner gloves (wool or synthetic)
☐ Vapor barrier (plastic socks or bags, etc.)

Clothing - Insulating Layer

☐ Pile shirts or jackets
☐ Down or fiberfill jackets
☐ Down or fiberfill vest
☐ Wool shirt
☐ Wool sweater
☐ Turtleneck
☐ Wool pants or knickers
☐ Pile pants
☐ Wool or pile socks (regular or knicker) (2 pairs)

☐ Wool stocking hat or balaclava
☐ Hood of jacket
☐ Mittens (wool or pile) (2 pairs)

Clothing - Protective Layer

☐ Windshirt or parka with hood
☐ Rain jacket
☐ Wind pants
☐ Overmittens

Other Clothing Items

☐ Suspenders, belt or webbing
☐ Bandana
☐ Face mask
☐ Gaiters

Pants Pockets

☐ Matches (in waterproof container)
☐ Knife
☐ Fire starter

Feet

☐ Ski boots
☐ Insoles
☐ Extra socks
☐ Boot wax
☐ Down or fiberfill booties
☐ Overboots

Skis and Accessories

- [ ] Skis and bindings
- [ ] Poles (screw together type for avalanche terrain)
- [ ] Skins or rope climbers

Haulage

- [ ] Pack
- [ ] Stuff bags with toggles

Bedroom

- [ ] Sleeping bag
- [ ] Sleeping pad
- [ ] Bivouac bag
- [ ] Vapor barrier inner bag
- [ ] Tent (poles, snow stakes, fly, guy lines)
- [ ] Candle or candle lantern

Kitchen

- [ ] Stove
- [ ] 12"x12" ensolite pad for insulation under stove
- [ ] Matches in stove
- [ ] Fuel bottle (with gas)
- [ ] Funnel
- [ ] Solid fuel pellets
- [ ] Pots
- [ ] Pot gripper
- [ ] Cup
- [ ] Spoon
- [ ] Corkscrew
- [ ] Food

Repair Kit

- [ ] Sewing needle
- [ ] Nylon thread or dental floss
- [ ] Duct tape
- [ ] Sheet metal (5"x2") - for pole repair
- [ ] Epoxy
- [ ] Screwdriver (posi-drive or regular) or screwdriver tip
- [ ] Vice grips (5" size)
- [ ] Extra screws to fit bindings
- [ ] Ski tip
- [ ] Clevis pins (for external frame packs)
- [ ] Bailing wire
- [ ] Cables for cable binding users
- [ ] Extra bails for pin binding users
- [ ] Extra basket
- [ ] Extra stove parts (gasket for *111-B* stove, fuel cap, etc.)

Emergency Kit

- [ ] Matches (in waterproof container)
- [ ] Fire starter (solid fuel pellets, candle, pitch wood, etc.)
- [ ] Compass
- [ ] Knife
- [ ] Whistle
- [ ] Nylon cord
- [ ] A couple of dimes

First Aid Kit

- ☐ Two gauze rolls (2" wide)
- ☐ Moleskin for blisters
- ☐ Chapstick
- ☐ Sunburn cream
- ☐ Two triangular bandages
- ☐ Six sterile pads (4"x4")
- ☐ Anti-acid tablets
- ☐ Ace bandage
- ☐ Bandaids—assorted sizes
- ☐ Butterfly closures
- ☐ Safety pins
- ☐ Aspirin
- ☐ Two-inch first aid tape
- ☐ First aid book
- ☐ Personal medications

Wax Kit

- ☐ Waxes (two-wax system or assorted waxes)
- ☐ Cork
- ☐ Scraper
- ☐ Wax remover (often overnight skiers will use white gas which is normally carried for stoves)
- ☐ Hand cleaner
- ☐ Rag

Avalanche Safety

- ☐ Pocket hand lens
- ☐ Shovel (2 per group)
- ☐ Avalanche beacon or avalanche cord

Personals

- ☐ Lotion
- ☐ Toothbrush/paste
- ☐ Glasses or contacts
- ☐ Comb
- ☐ Mirror

Miscellaneous

- ☐ Snow saw
- ☐ Sunglasses
- ☐ Goggles
- ☐ Headlamp or flashlight
- ☐ Extra candles
- ☐ Watch
- ☐ Notebook/pencil
- ☐ Book
- ☐ Wire saw
- ☐ Thermometer
- ☐ Toilet paper

CLOTHING

It may be hard to believe, but it is possible to be warm and comfortable when you are forty miles from the nearest electric heater and camping on ten feet of snow. This was not always true. I am convinced that a hundred years ago I couldn't have made a 200 mile ski across a wilderness area as comfortably as I did without advances in clothing and equipment that have taken place since then.

A few years ago when the energy crisis was beginning to attract public attention, several skiing friends and I organized a ski trek through the mountains surrounding our town. The idea was to interest the press and use the trip as a sounding board to express solutions for minimizing the use of energy. What better way than a demonstration to our community that tremendous opportunities for winter recreation exist right at its back door without people having to drive long distances.

Yuki, a Japanese climbing friend, planned to accompany us the first several days of the ten-day journey. It was early in January, and our progress was slowed by bitter winter winds and dropping temperatures. Yuki was cold during the day and things got worse at night. After supper, which was cooked while wrapped in our sleeping bags, Yuki crawled deep into his bag and disappeared from sight in a rip-stop nylon cocoon for the entire night. In the morning with the tent thickly covered by frost, everyone but Yuki began stirring. Eventually, his bag rustled a little and a hand appeared to accept some hot chocolate. Suddenly, he rocketed out of his sleeping bag. "Yuki, what's going on?" I asked. "I am leaving," he said simply and profoundly. Soon after, Yuki parted from our group and we watched him eagerly gliding toward the cluster of warm houses in the town below.

Yuke was smart. He wasn't comfortable. His clothing and sleeping bag weren't adequate for the temperatures. If you're not comfortable on a winter trip, there's no sense being there. Most of the rest of the party had adequate winter clothing and gear and were relatively snug. I have to qualify and say "relatively" since there were a couple of bitter days in the 25°-below-zero range when we were plain cold. There are some temperatures starting around 15° below zero and colder when I'd rather forget about winter camping and spend the evening in a cozy, wood-heated cabin drinking hot, spicy wine.

When you're not in a cozy cabin and are out somewhere on a backcountry trip, the idea is to be adequately prepared. Preparation begins at home. And since warmth is one of the primary considerations in winter camping, clothing comes first.

Air Space

Unless you wear electric socks, clothing doesn't produce heat. The body does. Clothing provides the insulation to keep heat trapped. Insulation traps air between clothing fibers or surrounding individual fibers. The more dead air space or more clothing you wear, the more effectively you'll be able to insulate yourself from the cold.

The dead air space must be dry to be most effective. Wet clothing doesn't insulate very well. The air spaces become clogged with water and insulating qualities are greatly reduced.

The most efficient method of putting this insulation over your body is in layers. When you become warmer while skiing, you can take off a layer. If you're still warm, you can remove another layer. Conversely, if you get colder, you can add a layer. If you don't wear layers and dress in only one thick layer, you'd probably cook while you're skiing and freeze when you take it off.

Clothing layers can be broken down into three categories: the protective layer on the outside, the insulating layer with all the bulk and the water vapor transfer or water vapor block layer. The water vapor transfer or block layer is the layer in which there are two entirely different clothing systems. These are the breathable and the vapor barrier systems.

A nylon shirt used as a vapor barrier.

Breathable System

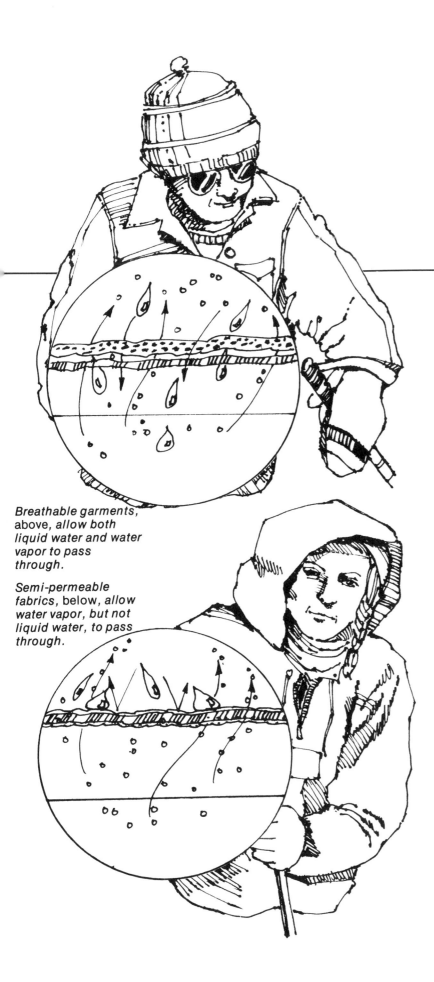

Breathable garments, above, allow both liquid water and water vapor to pass through.

Semi-permeable fabrics, below, allow water vapor, but not liquid water, to pass through.

The body is constantly giving off water vapor. You may have had the experience of sleeping in a bag after pulling a waterproof tarp over the top, only to wake and find your sleeping bag wet. The moisture came from your body. This water vapor is also called *insensible perspiration* or perspiration that you don't feel. In order to keep clothing from getting wet and losing its insulating qualities, the clothing layers should "breathe"—that is, allow water vapor to pass through to the outside. As long as it "breathes", you stay dry and warm. But if a waterproof layer is put on the *outside*, such as the waterproof tarp over the sleeping bag or a waterproof rain jacket over your clothing, then this moisture *cannot* pass through to the outside and, instead, condenses as water on your clothing.

A big breakthrough in waterproof yet breathable material has been a semi-permeable fabric called *Gore-Tex*. Other manufacturers have been or will be coming out with similar products. For lack of any general name for this material, I will call it semi-permeable fabric, because it allows water vapor, but not water, to pass through. It selectively permits water vapor molecules, which are relatively small, to pass through microscopic holes in the coating, while stopping liquid molecules, which are bonded to one another.

With this semi-permeable fabric in rain parkas, sleeping bag covers, and other clothing, you have the ability to keep dry from rain and melting snow while your body still "breathes".

Vapor Barrier System

The body gives off insensible perspiration as a means of keeping the skin comfortably humid. If the skin didn't have a surrounding layer of moisture, it would quickly dry and crack. Since cold air is relatively dry, the skin moisture evaporates easily and passes through the clothing to the outside. In the winter, the body pumps out insensible perspiration to keep the skin comfortable.

Evaporation of insensible perspiration cools the body. A vapor barrier, such as a plastic bag or coated nylon, placed over the skin blocks the water vapor and causes the humidity to rise within the trapped air until it reaches a comfortable level for the skin.

A plastic bag used as a vapor barrier on the feet.

For the feet, a common vapor barrier is a plastic bag. Yvon Chouinard, a famous ice climber and mountaineer, says he uses a thin wool sock, a plastic bag over it, a thick wool sock, and then another plastic bag. "You just can't keep your boots dry when climbing and bivouacking on a climb of several days," he says, "The plastic bag on the outside keeps my socks dry and the inner bag keeps my feet warm."

A vapor barrier inside a sleeping bag consists of a waterproofed, coated nylon bag of the same dimensions as the inside of the sleeping bag. "I can save weight by bringing my light down bag. I'd say the bag is 15° warmer with the vapor barrier," says Chouinard.

Preventing wetness in a vapor barrier system is a matter of *not* overheating. If you overheat, the body produces *sensible perspiration* or sweat. If you become overheated, then you would remove layers of clothing until comfortable. If you overheat in a vapor barrier sleeping bag, open the bag.

Insulation layers are still needed in a vapor barrier system. Wool shirts and down jackets are necessary to cover the vapor barrier shirt to provide needed insulation. Vapor barriers do not replace the need for insulation.

A vapor barrier keeps insulation dry and helps it retain its efficiency as insulation. Since the amount of perspiration is reduced through the use of a vapor barrier, dehydration is less of a problem than with breathable systems.

Combinations

A vapor barrier traps water vapor near the skin.

Like most items of equipment for outdoor use, skiers differ about what type of clothing is best for keeping warm. You may want to dabble a little and see what types of clothing work best for you. Our bodies perspire in different ways under differing conditions. Perhaps the best way of approaching winter clothing is to incorporate both systems in your winter wear. Chouinard uses a vapor barrier for his socks and sleeping bag, yet does not like the idea of vapor shirts or gloves.

Trying on a pile jacket in the shop.

Upper Body

In the breathable system, the layer of clothing next to the skin must transfer water vapor away from the skin through the other layers of clothing. Wool underwear has been the standard for years. Wool is used because it "breathes" well, allowing moisture to pass through. Wool doesn't absorb water readily and when it becomes damp, the moisture will move away from the skin so that the inner surface of the wool is drier against the skin.

Wipe off a window with a wool rag and a cotton rag. The wool rag does a very poor job of absorbing water. When wool gets wet, at least some insulation is still present. Some undershirts or long john combinations are made of beautiful Angora wool, some are mixtures of synthetics and others of cotton. The cotton combinations should be avoided because cotton holds water easily. Remember wiping the window. Unlike wool, cotton's air spaces are filled quickly with water and insulating qualities are reduced to nil.

Materials	Advantages	Disadvantages
cotton	Comfortable	Soaks in water readily. Air spaces become saturated and conduct cold.
wool	When wet, not all air spaces clog with water and this retains some heat. For years **the** standard of winter clothing.	Some people have allergies to wool. Some wools are scratchy. Wool is heavy and has a long drying time.
pile	Retains warmth when wet. Dries relatively quickly. Very comfortable. Feels instantly warm. Light.	Bulky. Requires large stuff bags. Loft reduced in some piles when washed. Wind can blow through easily.
olefin polypropylene	Provides excellent water vapor transfer as sock liners and underwear.	Some skiers do not like silky feel.
synthetic fiberfill	Fibers absorb very little water. Retains loft when wet. Dries relatively quickly.	Bulkier and heavier than down. Wears out and loses loft quicker than well-cared-for down clothes.
down	Light. Easily compressible. Comfortable.	Looses loft dramatically if it becomes wet. Difficult to dry.

Many skiers are turning to synthetics. Some of the finest synthetics for underwear are those made of materials like olefin and polypropylene. These materials can move water vapor quickly to the outside clothing layers and are comfortable to wear.

Pile underwear, which is made of acrylic fibers processed to give a springy and furry appearance, are preferred by some skiers because of its comfort and feeling of immediately warming up the body.

The insulating layers for the upper body can be wool shirts, wool sweaters, down vests, pile shirts and jackets. I can't say enough about pile. It serves as a synthetic replacement for wool. It is lighter than wool and dries much more quickly than wool.

Other insulating garments include down jackets or jackets insulated with synthetic fiberfills such as *PolarGuard, Hollofill* and *Thinsulate.*

The advantages of some of the most widely used insulating materials are summarized in the chart.

The protective layers over the upper

body should stop the wind from blowing through the insulating clothing layers and cooling you. To prevent chilling from wind, skiers typically use nylon wind jackets or shells. In wet snow conditions or rain, which can happen even in the powder kingdom of the West, rain parkas or cagoules (a rain parka that hangs to the knees) are very advantageous. Remember, bring clothing that will keep insulation dry.

I don't believe I've ever been on a trip where any one clothing combination predominated. One possible upper body combination for standing around in cold conditions might be a wool undershirt, wool and synthetic turtleneck, pile shirt, and a down jacket. Another combination might be a polypropylene undershirt, wool shirt, wool sweater, and a fiberfill parka. When you're skiing with a pack on your back and working hard, the clothing you'll need is significantly reduced. Often, all I wear is an undershirt and a wind shell. In windy conditions on a ridge, I might wear a wool or synthetic undershirt, wool shirt, and wind shell.

Here are a few features that you may look for when purchasing or sewing shirts and parkas:

- Pockets are handy. Since wind shells are commonly used while traveling during the day, lots of pockets, or at least one large pocket, are very helpful. The large pocket can keep your map easily accessible. Other clothing items should have pockets. They are useful for stuffing matches, compass, fire starter, and litter found along the trail. *Velcro* closures on the pocket make it easy to get in them wearing mittens.

- A good parka will have draw strings to draw it closer into the body when the weather is windy. Some parkas have a powder flap around the waist on the inside, which prevents snow from getting in if you fall.

- Collars on most wool shirts are for looks rather than function. *Petzoldt Wilderness Equipment* makes a collar on a wool shirt that can be fastened into a turtleneck. This helps keep your neck warm. Some pile shirts have a large collar that can be zipped up to form a turtleneck extending partly up the chin.

- When dressing in layers for cold, subzero temperatures, most of the layers are usually sized to fit. The outer layers, however, will probably be one size larger than you normally wear. I normally wear a "medium," but by the time I put on synthetic underwear, wool shirt, and a pile jacket, my last layer of a down jacket or a wind parka will be size "large."

Legs

Skiers use a variety of clothing for the lower body. Most common are wool long johns underneath wool pants. Good wool pants are available at cross-country speciality shops, or sometimes can be found at surplus or used clothing stores. Clean them before the trip, otherwise you can end up smelling of moth balls. Synthetics such as olefin and polypropylene provide a good vapor transport layer next to the skin.

Pile pants are being used more and more by skiers in cold conditions. Some backcountry skiers use the traditional knickers which allow freedom of movement but also necessitate carrying heavier knicker socks. Stretch nylon pants are used by some, although the pockets are usually too small and tight.

For the protective layer, wind pants are common. Buy them loose enough for the complete range of movement you'll need. Some skiers will ski in their long johns and wind pants, and in the evening put on wool or pile pants for warmth.

Gaiters are vital for the backcountry skier since they keep snow from working into the boot. Long, knee-length gaiters, while cumbersome, are preferred by many backcountry skiers. Short gaiters will do the job. Zip gaiters are the most convenient since they can be easily slipped on and taken off. If you buy a pair, make sure there is a snap or *Velcro* flap which covers the zipper to keep packed snow or ice from freezing on the zipper and making it difficult to zip. I had a friend who after a cold night had a zipper full of ice and could not get his gaiters off. Finally, in desperation, he took a match to the nylon zipper to melt the ice. As you can imagine, the match did more than melt the ice. *Snow Seal* put on the zipper will help to keep ice from forming. The better gaiters are waterproofed at the bottom to give added water protection to the boots. The upper part of the gaiter can be waterproof or breathable depending on your preference.

Belts are worn by many skiers to keep their pants up. I have a difficult time, however, when I'm wearing a heavy pack with a belt since it tends to rub my lower back. Some solve this problem by using webbing. I use suspenders.

Feet

The layer principle is also applied to feet though it is impossible to remove and add layers during the day. A thin liner sock should be worn closest to the skin. The liner sock can be a thin wool or an olefin sock. The synthetics such as olefin have a smooth texture that many skiers swear reduces friction against the foot and minimizes blisters.

Most skiers seal their boots to keep the feet dry in soggy snow conditions. But, sealing the boots will block water vapor produced by the feet. On longer tours, the water vapor condenses in the boot leather and socks, gradually soaking the insulation from the inside. Boots freeze and become stiff during a cold night and the insulating qualities of the socks are reduced. To prevent this, skiers can wear a thin, inner sock, then a plastic bag as a vapor barrier. Some companies like *Wigwam* make a plastic sock. The normal thick wool sock is worn over the plastic. In addition, more plastic can be worn as a final layer over the thick wool sock. This will protect the sock from any water that may seep through the boot.

Feet are important since they get cold first, and they get cold when not being used. One bitterly cold morning, I packed quickly and got on the trail immediately before my feet got too cold. My partner was a woman law student who, after a long inactive semester, was ready for some exercise. I raced down the trail. After a long period of vigorous skiing, my feet began to warm up. Satisfied, but weary from the skiing, I looked around to see

*Putting on overboots
in camp.*

54

how far Ellen was behind after my blistering pace. But she was right behind me, looking fresh and eager for more.

When arriving at camp at night, damp socks should be changed to dry socks. For comfort and warmth, down or fiberfill booties can't be beat. Slip in a piece of ensolite or shoe inserts to increase the warmth of down booties. You'll want to have one to two inches of insulation between your foot and the ground to keep warm. For further warmth and the ability to walk around in snow while preparing the camp, bring a pair of overboots that can be pulled over the down booties. A friend uses his overboots as stuff sacks in his pack. Using this type of foot wear for camp use can make all the difference in comfort in the evenings.

Hands

One of the most practical items for hand wear is a liner glove. Silk liner gloves are available but the synthetics such as olefin are more common. There's a type of synthetic liner glove that has a metallic sheen that has been on the market for Alpine skiers and works well for cross-country skiing. The synthetic liners are so thin that you can light a stove, tie a knot in nylon cord or use a camera. I wear my liners even on warm winter days, just to keep my hands from drying and cracking.

Gloves can be worn over the liners. Wool gloves are the most common. Usually, it's best to stay away from leather gloves since they soak up water and become worthless for insulation and difficult to dry out.

For really keeping the fingers warm, you'll want mittens. Thick wool mittens sometimes called Dachstein mitts or thick pile mittens are the best way to go. You can wear synthetic liners inside the mittens which give you an extra layer for warmth and are there when you need them.

A protective overmitten is very helpful. Overmittens usually have waterproof palms, breathable backs, and keep the wool mitts dry and protected from wind. I'll also use my overmittens when it is too warm to wear wool mittens, and too cool to wear only my liner gloves.

Using nylon mittens as a protective shell.

Head

Providing insulation for the head and neck is critical since almost two-thirds of the body's heat can be lost from this area. Wool stocking hats or balaclavas that can be pulled down to the neck are the most common. Don't wash them in hot water. I've learned the hard way. Some folks are returning to the use of older types with ear flaps and visors which shield the face from the sun and falling snow.

For very cold weather and wind, you'll want a hood on your fiberfill, down, or pile jacket. When buying parkas, make sure the hood will fit comfortably over your wool hat. Many are not cut full enough to do this.

A neckerchief is a common item for many skiers. It serves a variety of uses from wind protection on the face, to wiping off sun glasses, to tying as a triangular bandage, to picking up hot pots. On really cold trips in severe areas, you may want to use a face mask which protects the face from bitter winds.

Possible Clothing Combinations

	Inside Layer		Insulating Layer	Protective Layer
torso and arms	BREATHABLE: Wool underwear shirt; net underwear; synthetic, i.e., polypropylene undershirts.	VAPOR BARRIER: Vapor shirt (waterproof nylon), alone or with undershirt.	Wool shirt, sweater; turtleneck; pile shirt or jacket; down/fiberfill vest or jacket; foamback jacket.	Wind shield or parka; rain parka.
legs	BREATHABLE: Wool pants, knickers or long johns; synthetic long johns.	VAPOR BARRIER: Waterproof pants.	Wool pants or knickers; pile pants.	Nylon or *Gore-Tex* wind pants.
feet	BREATHABLE: Synthetic (olefin) liner socks; thin wools.	VAPOR BARRIER: Plastic bags/socks with thin liners.	Wool or pile socks.	For vapor barrier, plastic bag/socks go over wool socks.
hands	BREATHABLE: Silk, synthetic (olefin), or wool liners.	VAPOR BARRIER: Plastic gloves.	Wool gloves or mittens; pile mittens.	Overmittens, nylon or *Gore-Tex*.
head			Wool stocking cap or balaclava; fiberfill/ down/pile hood; ear band.	Wind shell or parka hood.
neck			Turtleneck; scarf or neckerchief.	

FOOD

On a cold December night of my first overnight backcountry trip, four of us were wrapped in our sleeping bags watching Harrison Hilbert, whom we called "H", prepare the night's supper. "H" used his funnel and poured a generous quantity of white gas into his 111-B stove. After replacing the cap, he pursed his lips and vigorously pumped the stove. The fuel seeped out, filled the little cup at the base of the vaporizing tube, and spilled over into the metal box containing the stove. He lit a match, leaned back, and whooomph! The entire tent flashed while the rest of us dove for protection. "H" nonchalantly set a pot of snow on the stove as the fumes settled down.

Supper consisted of thoroughly boiled, undrained macaroni and cheese and the contents of an assortment of beat-up packages on which the names could no longer be ascertained. They looked as if they had been jostling in his pack for several years.

Ah, finally it was done. We held out our cups as he shoveled and shook spoonfuls of the steaming, sticky mass into our cups. Even with lots of water to wash it down, it was terrible; and the faint taste of white gas fumes stayed with me the rest of the trip. That was the last time "H" cooked. From then on, we eagerly volunteered to do all the cooking.

The rumor in those days was that "H" never liked to cook and always started a trip by cooking the first meal. He never worried about cooking after that. At any rate, "H" has improved over the years, and he's now an exquisite cook, especially known for his tasty beer biscuits.

With more finesse, however, "H's" use of the one-pot meal is a sound one for ski camping. Except when there is the convenience of a warm snow cave or igloo, you will want meals that are quick and easy. Time is limited in the winter and winter travel burns up a tremendous amount of calories. After arriving in camp, you will begin to cool off, and the sooner you can drink warm liquids and eat a hot meal, the more comfortable and refreshed you will feel. So plan your suppers around the one-pot meal. Lunches which are eaten along the trail should consist of food that you don't have to cook, such as cheese, raisins, and salami. Breakfasts should also be geared to warming up quickly to start the day with a pleasant, glowing feeling.

Nutrition

The number of calories burned on a backcountry trip start at around 4,000 a day and can jump considerably when days are colder and skiing is strenuous. In order to keep up with this high level of caloric output, a skier must eat plenty of food, especially foods with high caloric values. It is essential to continue to eat snacks throughout the day in addition to hearty breakfasts and suppers. The energy that gets you through a day of skiing, hauling a pack, and keeping you warm at night, is largely supplied by trip food eaten on the trip. If you're not eating enough, skiing will be more exhausting. You'll also get cold easier, leading to uncomfortable nights and perhaps even to hypothermia. Don't worry about your weight. I've never known anyone who has gained weight on a backcountry trip. In fact, a backcountry ski trip is a good way to shave off a few unwanted pounds.

Seldom will skiers sit down with the Department of Agriculture's *Composition of Foods* and figure out the caloric values of trip food from the major food groups: carbohydrates, fats, and proteins. How much intake you need from each group varies from source to source, but here are some guidelines: At least 50 percent of the food should consist of carbohydrates, such as pastas, vegetables (especially starchy types), grains, cereals, fruits, and candy with sugar or honey. Go very heavy on fats since this is where you pick up more calories per weight than any other food group. Fats are more efficiently used by the body if they are accompanied by a high portion of carbohydrates. Fat comes from margarine or butter added to meals, nuts, peanut butter, cheese, salami, and canned fish. Proteins, of course, are important but play less of a role. Proteins can be obtained from such foods as meats, cheese, and milk.

Besides caloric needs, the body loses tremendous amounts of fluid by "insensible" loss, through perspiration, and through the lungs while breathing. Because cold air is dryer than warm air, the loss of fluids is more acute. Evaporation of bodily fluids takes place at a more rapid rate than on summer trips. Drinking several quarts of water each day is vital since a skier can be slowly dehydrating himself and not even realize it. Force liquids; you won't always be thirsty. You will feel better and be more energetic if you do. Keep an eye on your urine. If it looks dark, due to concentration, you may not be getting enough water.

Along with water loss, the body loses salts like sodium and potassium that are together called electrolytes. Some skiers use salt tablets, but it is debatable whether it is really necessary if you are eating substantial meals. The body's needs are normally met by seasoning with salt and the natural amounts found in foods. Other electrolytes are obtained from meats, nuts, dried fruit, and raisins. Some skiers like special electrolyte drinks which are designed to replace lost salts. These drinks, such as *ERG* or *Body Punch*, can be found at cross-country ski shops and sporting goods stores.

Breakfast

Lunch

Plan breakfast foods which are quick and easy to make:

Start with a hot drink. . .
  hot cocoa
  coffee
  tea
  hot jello
  hot fruit drinks (*Kool Aid, Wylers*)
  hot carob

Then, the breakfast...
  granola (various recipes are available
    from cookbooks)
  quick-cooking cereals (throw in nuts
    or dried fruits to give them more
    caloric value)
  instant breakfasts
  instant soups
  breakfast squares
  instant potatoes and butter
  boiled rehydrated fruits (these can be
  jazzed up by adding *Bisquick* to
  make a type of fruit cobbler)
  lunch and snack foods

Lunches are eaten along the trail. They can supplement breakfasts and suppers, or sometimes they are used in the place of supper or breakfast. Bring lunch food that doesn't have to be cooked.

Drinks. . .
  fruit drinks (*Kool Aid, Wylers*)
  dried milk
  electrolyte drinks (*ERG, Body Punch*)

Lunch Suggestions:
  sausage or salami (dried type of
    salami won't freeze as badly)
  jerky
  canned fish (tuna, sardines, kippers)
  dried or smoked meats
  cheese
  crackers
  nuts
  raisins
  dried fruits (apples, banana chips,
    dates, pears, peaches, figs)
  compact breads and biscuits
  candies (homemade or commercial:
    chocolate bars, hard candies, gran-
    ola bars, space sticks)
  cookies and fudge

Supper

The easiest supper is a freeze-dried meal. There are different types of freeze-dried foods on the market according to the way they are to be prepared, so be sure to read the directions before buying. Some have cooking procedures requiring several steps: pre-soaking of certain ingredients, combining several packages, and the preparation of some of the ingredients in separate pots. Avoid this variety. If you have to go to all of that trouble to make a meal as well as having to pay the extra expense for freeze-dried food, you might as well buy fresh food from the supermarket.

The best freeze-dried meals are one-step operations. You simply add boiling water and wait a few minutes for it to soak all ingredients. When you are moving every day, it's cold, and you need to be able to serve supper quickly. Freeze-dried foods fulfill this winter camping requirement.

Filling up an insulated water bottle.

The problem with freeze-dried foods is that they are expensive. There are, however, several ways of saving money. Some companies offer bulk prices. You may be able to divide the cost among friends and place a large order, enough to keep you supplied for all of the trips that winter. Some companies offer freeze-dried food in #10 cans which are even cheaper when bought in bulk. I've used the #10 can system for several long ski journeys. One #10 can will provide a hearty meal for four skiers. Before leaving on the trip, open the can and put its contents in a plastic bag.

Another way to save money is to make your own food. Dehydrators are easy to build and can be used to dry jerky, vegetables, and fruits. With this method, the cooking times are longer than for freeze-dried items. Several books are available that describe home drying. If you are the tinkering type, it is possible to construct your own freeze drier.

Many fine meals can be made by buying basic ingredients at the grocery store and by combining pastas, grains, meats, and vegetables. The following chart can aid in planning meals. Pick one

One Pot Meal Chart

Grains, Pastas and Other Bases	Meats	Meat Substitutes	Vegetables	Garnishes
Macaroni egg and wheat	Freeze-dried or dehydrated meat	Canned meat substitutes vegie-links, vegetable scallops, beef, turkey and chicken	Freeze-dried or dehydrated vegetables beans, carrots, peas, tomatos, corn	Sunflower seeds
Spaghetti egg and wheat	Canned fish sardines, shrimp, tuna, kippers, anchovies, crab meat, oysters, clams	Texturized vegetable protein	Vegetable flakes and dices onion, celery, mushrooms and green peppers	Chopped nuts almonds, peanuts, cashews, walnuts
Noodles egg and wheat				Sesame seeds
Ramen noodles	Canned meats turkey, chicken, liverwurst, corn beef, Spam	Cheese		Soy beans
Rice		Vegetable bacon bits		Chia seeds
Instant Potatoes				Kelp
Bulgar	Canned sausages			
Buckwheat	Jerky			Brewers yeast "primary grown"
Instant Soup *Liptons, Cup of Soup*, natural soup mixes	Salami			Wheat germ
	Sausages			Raisins and dried fruits
Broth Mixes meat and natural	Bacon bar or bits			
Bullion Cubes				
Instant Sauces				

64

Convenience Foods

or more items from each column and combine together for a one-pot meal.

Seasoning can mean the difference between a tasty one-pot meal and one that is blah. Bring along several seasonings and spices which can be carried in plastic containers or film cans. Salt, pepper, vegetable seasoning such as *Vegit*, cayenne pepper, chili pepper, oregano and garlic will add zip to an ordinary supper.

Supper should begin with a hot drink or some instant soup. While people are sipping their drinks, chatting, and warming up, more snow can be melted and the main course prepared. After supper, more hot drinks can be prepared, and perhaps a treat like popcorn or pudding. Other desserts like cookies and fudges (there's an excellent peanut butter fudge recipe in *Simple Foods for the Pack,* by Vikki Kinmont and Claudia Axcell, Sierra Club, page 49) can be prepared at home and carried along with the lunch items. Keep melting snow and warming water until everyone is full. The best time to replenish lost liquids is during and after supper. Add a spoonful of butter or margarine to food and even drinks. It will taste good when you are in this condition and it adds a needed boost of calories.

When George over at the Organic Grocery sees this book, he'll have a fit. Many of the suggested food items are processed, bleached, and filled with various chemicals and preservatives. Eating whole food is a real problem on backcountry ski trips. The nature of convenience foods - quick, easy to prepare and quick cooking - make them ideal for winter camping when it's cold and fuel is limited.

Natural Foods

Some skiers who are careful with their diet make a compromise while winter camping hoping that their day of vigorous exercise will somehow balance some of the harmful effects of food additives.

For those who can't compromise their diet, it is possible to purchase natural freeze-dried foods. It is also possible, using the one-pot meal chart shown here, to make one-pot meals from items purchased at the supermarket and organic grocery store. Generally, however, you will have to plan on longer cooking times, and thus consume more fuel.

White sugar can be eliminated by substituting honey or by making or buying granola bars and fudges made with honey. Other honey candy bars can be purchased at organic groceries. Honey can be used on breakfast cereals, but it will become very stiff in winter temperatures. Carry honey in a plastic container which you can put in the pot of water while it's heating on the stove. Be sure to have some quick-energy food containing honey for those cold, wet, or energy-sapping days.

If you are a vegetarian, you must plan meals carefully. At least one Outward Bound School doesn't allow vegetarian diets on their winter courses. Most of their hypothermia cases have involved vegetarians. It can be done and vegetarian diets are used by skiers all the time, but you must use caution. Keep a close eye on calories and make sure you are packing a lot of food value in the foods you decide to bring.

Fuel for the Stove

Packing

If you have four people in your party and are melting snow for water and meals, figure on a gallon of fuel plus a tank of gas for each week. That's a little more than one pint of fuel per day for four skiers. If there are two skiers in the party, cut that figure in half. If you are going solo, plan your fuel needs the same as for two people.

If you've brought plenty of fats, 2¼ to 2½ pounds of food per day will give you 4,000-plus calories. Weights of foods per day are less for those packing freeze-dried foods.

Avoid squeeze tubes (*Gerry Tubes*) in the winter. They freeze and there's no way to get the contents out unless you put the tube in boiling water. Plastic bottles, especially those with a rubber gasket on the lid, are excellent for items like honey and peanut butter.

Other dried foods can be packaged in plastic bags. Some skiers prefer zip-lock bags; others use regular plastic bags. Freezer bags are thicker and stronger and preferred by still others. Freeze-dried food can be removed from foil packages before the onset of the trip and packaged in plastic bags to save weight. If you have different ingredients for an evening's supper, pre-mix them at home, and put it all in the same plastic bag. Take care of all of the food hassles at home so cooking on the trip is easier.

ON THE TRAIL

Newspaper reporters in the mining towns of the late 1800's couldn't resist an occasional snide remark about the unwieldly nature of long snowshoes, as skis were called. This is what one reporter had to say in the December 23, 1865, issue of the Silver City, Idaho, newspaper:

Snow-shoes are a noticeable feature in traveling now-a-days, and many are the tumbles incident to the inexperienced. Yesterday, we saw an enthusiastic hombre, passing our office, going through some motions that would compel the India-rubber man to take down his bills. One shoe stuck perpendicular in the road, while the other went through the wood pile and clinched; his head was dovetailed between a two-board fence, while his legs, sticking out of the snow, gave him the appearance of having made a dive for China, and with such force as to cause us to believe him, for a moment, 'one of the elect' for some other more tropical clime this side. Such maneuvers on tolerably level ground only show what the man could do on a mountain side. Give the man a chance.

Despite the humorous situations the early skier sometimes encountered, skis were often an essential means of winter-time transportation through the snowy, western mountains. Mail was carried on skis in Colorado including one route over an 11,000-foot pass between the towns of Georgetown and Hot Sulphur Springs. In Idaho, some miners were known to ski over a hundred miles through the snowbound central part of the state to try their luck at a new gold discovery. And blue-eyed, blond-haired John Arthur Thompson established the only means of East-West communication across the California Sierras with a 90-mile mail route between Placerville in California and Carson Valley in Nevada.

With their long, heavy skis (Thompson had a pair made of oak that weighed 25 pounds), some of the early skiers could ski 30 to 40 miles a day in favorable conditions with heavy canvas packs on their backs. One notable aspect of their technique on long tours was pacing. Without a steady, even pace, they would never have been able to ski all day and sometimes all night across North America's great wilderness.

Ski trail, California.

Fletcher Manley

Pace

When you first leave the trailhead, it takes a while to adjust to being out in snow country again. Whether the weather is good or bad, the whole change of environment from your home, to highway driving, to a pocket of wild country, provides new stimulus to your mind and senses. And it takes time to absorb the newness and to slow down to the pace of nature around you.

Usually, skiing begins with a burst of energy. Pent-up excitement finds a way out now that the journey is underway. If that's the way you feel, let it happen. Ski hard for a while. When you're feeling more in tune, more relaxed, settle down into your pace.

You should know about pacing yourself from day trips. The pace slows down more with a pack on your back. Establish a pace that you can maintain all day. If you have to rest, your pace is too fast. Rest stops should not be taken for the sake of resting for short spurts of energy. Instead,

they should be used to give your shoulders a break, to get a snack, or to shed or add clothes. If you're resting because of exhaustion, the pace is much too fast.

At the beginning of any trip, there's a break-in period. You'll find yourself stopping to take off a jacket, to adjust the pack, to put moleskin on a sore spot on your foot, to wax slippery skis, or to tie on equipment falling off your pack. You'll make frequent stops for all those little things that make you feel like you're standing with a load of packages on a crowded city bus that has to make stops at every other corner on the way home. Hang in there. Find your stride and don't plan too many miles the first day.

When you are standing around on a winter day, you'll be all bundled up in layers of clothing. Soon after you get moving, the body begins to warm up. Just as you feel this warming, take off a layer of clothing. Sometimes you only need to take off a hat. Other times, it means stopping, taking off your pack, and removing a jacket or wool shirt. It is crucial to avoid overheating. Overheating means sweat, and sweat absorbed into breathable clothing means that some of its insulating qualities will be lost. If you're using a vapor barrier shirt, it means it will get wet, clammy, and uncomfortable.

An overheated body becomes inefficient and overtired. Anticipate body warmth and remove clothing layers right away. The only exception is if you have cold feet or hands. In that case, leave on your layers until feet and hands warm up.

You may find yourself removing so many layers that you're down to an undershirt. When skiers have reached their steady pace, they often will travel with an upper layer of only an undershirt and windbreaker. It can be an invigorating feeling in the cool air.

When you stop, your body will begin to cool. Again, try to *anticipate* becoming cool and put on layers before you get chilled. Remember this general principle: once you are warm, it's easy to stay warm; once you are cold, it's a hard job to get warm again.

Be fastidious and fanatical about staying dry. Watch overheating which can wet clothing from the inside. Brush snow off clothing. Put on a parka when it's snowing.

Rest Stops

Groups

The ultimate source of energy is the combustion of glucose with oxygen to form carbon dioxide. But we don't get a lot of oxygen while exercising. During those times, the conversion of glucose to lactic acid provides some energy without using any oxygen. But if lactic acid accumulates, muscles tire quickly. We need oxygen to combine with the glucose or else it converts to lactic acid. That is why we should pace ourselves with steady breathing while skiing.

Keep rest stops brief. The greatest amount of lactic acid is removed from your muscles during the first several minutes of a rest as your body recovers from exertion. Thereafter, the percentage of lactic acid removed drops considerably. Longer rests, therefore, aren't going to be that beneficial from a physiological standpoint.

It's also hard to get yourself going psychologically after a long break, particularly if you're going to be facing the uncomfortable prospect of more strenuous exercise.

While traveling in groups, you should stay in sight of each other. If you are in a safe area, it's fine for your group to spread out. After all, it's sometimes nice to ski by yourself. But always maintain some contact. If you are in the lead, stop and wait occasionally; make sure everyone in the party is still together, then continue on. When traveling, be conscious of the person behind you. Always keep checking to see if he is there. This casual "buddy" system can prevent a lot of problems.

When traveling in dangerous areas—steep terrain, thick timber, storms, or where it's easy to get lost—it is vital to keep everyone together.

The fastest members of the group should adjust their pace to that of the slowest members. Slower skiers should ski at their comfortable pace. If you get tired, call for a rest. This should immediately indicate to the faster members that the pace is too fast and that they need to slow down. Causing slower skiers to ski at a faster pace only invites fatigue and weakens the party in the long run.

Leading

The smartest procedure that any group can follow is to allow all members of the party a chance to lead and break trail, even if it's only for a few hundred feet.

It's a psychological boost to lead for a while, especially when you are breaking trail. Leading makes everyone feel as if they're contributing to the group effort and gives a greater common sense of purpose. Letting the slower skier up front even for a short while raises spirits and morale.

The phenomenon of the psychological boost while leading is an interesting one to watch. It's especially evident when approaching the tops of ridges or passes where the sense of accomplishment and excitement runs high.

In self-led groups, everyone is working together for the success of the trip. Everyone has a responsibility to assess how the other members of the group are doing. No one should be pushed to exhaustion. If it means camping early, do it. The hard-core skiers who haven't gotten enough exercise can dig igloos and snowcaves or cut turns on nearby slopes.

Water

Breaking Trail

Drink as much water as possible. Fruit juice mixes added to the water make it tasty and easier to drink. Snow can be added to partially full water bottles and, eventually, if the temperatures aren't too cold, you'll have more water. Wrap your water bottle in a piece of ensolite to keep it insulated from the cold. In colder conditions, some skiers hang a *bota* bag under their shirt so water doesn't freeze. Drink plenty in the morning and at night. Remember, there are no faucets along the way.

Breaking trail through powder or wet, heavy snow is tiring. There are several methods for using the full resources of your party:

- Leap frogging. The lead skier breaks until he begins to get tired (not exhausted) and then allows the next in line to take over. Sometimes this may be only a few hundred feet. The leader steps off to the side and waits until the last person has passed him and then falls into single file at the end of the line. Skiing on broken trail is easier and less taxing, and by the time this person reaches the front again, he is refreshed and ready to break trail.

- One of the members of the party splits up the contents of his pack among the rest of the party. He then breaks trail until he starts getting tired. After a while, he switches his empty pack with someone else and a new person breaks trail.

- One of the members of the party leaves his pack on the trail and skis ahead breaking trail. When he tires, he returns over the broken trail to retrieve his pack. Another member leaves his pack where the first skier left off and takes the lead. The problem with this method is that it spreads the party out. It shouldn't be used in avalanche terrain.

Wildlife

During the winter, animals are in their most critical time for survival. Life sustaining food is scarce and during some winters food may be barely available. Big game are bogged down by snow and move slowly from place to place.

Ski parties which cause big game to run and expend vital energy reserves can actually endanger the animals' lives. If you encounter game on a trip, always observe them from a distance. Dogs are particularly bothersome to game and should be left at home.

R. Hamilton Smith

Mink on ice, Wisconsin.

Greg Pole

Elk.

Awareness

As you are traveling, always be alert to what is happening around you. Anybody getting tired? What landmarks are guiding your way? Any avalanche danger? Will it be windy on the ridge you are approaching? What happens if someone gets injured—what's the best way out? Enjoy the day and have fun but always think ahead. There are no absolute rules in the winter wilderness. You and your party will have to depend on common sense and good judgment based on your awareness and previous experiences.

For those unexpected nights of travel, bring a headlamp along. It permits skiing with full use of your arms and is invaluable around camp when you need free hands to do chores.

Night skiing with headlamp.

Basic Stride

The basic backcountry stride is sliding along. Your arms should be kept low. Use the arms to help you glide along but not to the point where they become fatigued. Poles should be angled back and positioned wider than track touring to provide balance. Avoid bobbing and wobbling by your upper body since it wastes energy. The movements should be relaxed.

In powder conditions or anytime you are breaking through snow, push the tip of the ski up and forward so the tip rises to the top of the snow. This is preferable to pushing through the snow under the surface. In loose snow, it may help to think of your toes controlling your skis. To clear your tip, push your toes up.

Stream
Crossing

The easiest method of getting to the other side of a stream is to cross a snow bridge covering the stream. Look for a bridge that seems sturdy. In the spring, try to time stream crossings for the mornings when snow bridges are frozen. Take hands

out of pole straps and release the waist strap on the pack so you can get out of your pack quickly in case the bridge gives away. Ski gingerly near the bridge. Probe it with your pole. If it feels safe, cross it with skis wide apart and with smooth, even strides.

If there are no snow bridges, look for fallen logs. Some thick logs can be crossed by walking if the snow is not excessively slippery. Lash skis to the pack and use the poles for balancing.

If the log is too slippery, lash skis to the pack, straddle the log and shinny across it on your rear. Sometimes it may be necessary to use a shovel and knock the snow off the log in front of you as you cross. The poles can be used for balance.

If there are no snow bridges or logs, the only method left is to ford. If you know in advance that you'll be fording, it is a good idea to bring tennis shoes or thongs in order to keep your boots dry, and make the crossing much more comfortable. If you have no tennis shoes with you, wear a pair of spare socks without boots. Otherwise, you will have to go barefoot which can be shaky when you've got a heavy load. Tie skis to the pack and use poles as balance. Move across the stream steadily and carefully. Face upstream if the current is strong enough to undermine your position.

Carrying Skis

There are a number of different ways to carry skis:

- Lash both skis and poles to the pack.
- Lash only the skis to the pack and use the poles for balance.
- Slip the basket over the tip of the ski and clip the pole shaft under the bail of the pin bindings. With this method, the ski and pole become one unit. You can hold the pole as a handle. This is a good way to carry skis when you've removed them for a short stretch and don't want to take off your pack to fasten them on.
- Both skis and poles can be lashed together. Reverse the poles with the basket of one near the handle of the other. Slip them over the skis which have been placed bottom to bottom. Place each pole's handle strap just above the other pole's basket and tighten the straps. The poles can be used as a handle.

Bushwacking

The problem with trying to get through a tangle of trees and brush is that your skis keep sliding into branches and getting caught. A way of handling this situation is to make your skis into snowshoes. Strap on some rope climbers which prevent slipping and make it easier to get through brush.

Waxing

No temperatures are indicated in the waxing chart below, as skiers usually don't have time to take temperatures. A rough but accurate measure is to grab a handful of snow and check how it reacts to your mitten.

Brand names have been eliminated (except in the case of two-wax systems) since the widely used waxes follow the same color key. Many skiers will bring a selection of hard waxes and substitute the warm wax of a two-wax system for klister. The following definitions will help in using the chart:

- New snow - snow in the process of falling or within the last day or day and a half.
- Settled snow - snow which had been on the ground for a while, approximately more than a day and a half.
- Melted and frozen snow - corn, ice crust, granular snow.

Backcountry Waxing Chart

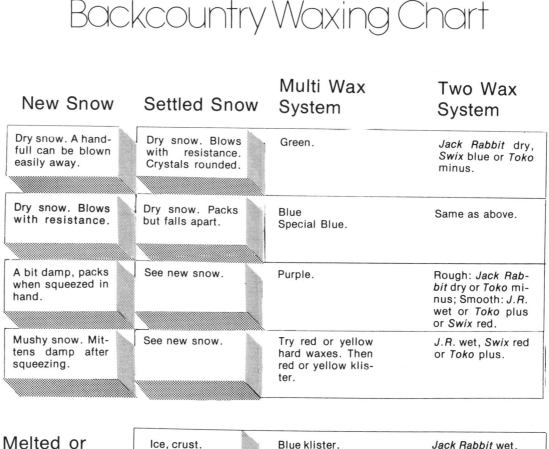

New Snow	Settled Snow	Multi Wax System	Two Wax System
Dry snow. A handfull can be blown easily away.	Dry snow. Blows with resistance. Crystals rounded.	Green.	*Jack Rabbit* dry, *Swix* blue or *Toko* minus.
Dry snow. Blows with resistance.	Dry snow. Packs but falls apart.	Blue Special Blue.	Same as above.
A bit damp, packs when squeezed in hand.	See new snow.	Purple.	Rough: *Jack Rabbit* dry or *Toko* minus; Smooth: *J.R.* wet or *Toko* plus or *Swix* red.
Mushy snow. Mittens damp after squeezing.	See new snow.	Try red or yellow hard waxes. Then red or yellow klister.	*J.R.* wet, *Swix* red or *Toko* plus.

Melted or Refrozen Snow		Multi Wax System	Two Wax System
	Ice, crust.	Blue klister.	*Jack Rabbit* wet, *Swix* red or *Toko* plus.
	Crust becoming mushy, corn, coarse snow.	Purple klister.	Same as above.
	Wet, Slushy, rotting snow.	Red/silver klister.	Same as above.

Waxing Odds and Ends

• Where you are going will affect what type of wax you use. If you will be climbing most of the day, you will probably want softer wax to provide a good, secure grip. If you're descending, you'll want to use a harder wax.

• Many backcountry skiers don't worry about kickers in backcountry skiing, especially with fiberglass skis. As backcountry technique, for the most part, is sliding along, moving at a much slower paced than when on a track, the extra grip of a fully waxed ski will be helpful. Those who do use a kicker usually wax their skis for about 3½ feet.

• Transition snow around the 32° F (0°) range is a very difficult snow condition to wax for. The snow on the top is warm and the snow underneath is cold. The cold snow freezes; the warm snow sticks to skis and causes them to ice and collect clumps of snow. This is a good time to use skins. But if you don't have them, try waxing for the colder, powder snow first. If that doesn't work, try a little softer wax but apply like a crayon in patches on the ski.

Sometimes if a ski is icing up, you can add streaks of paraffin or glide wax. Other methods include putting a "cushion" on the bottom of the ski. This can be done by applying a blue klister, letting it harden, and then applying a hard wax such as blue over the top of the klister. The klister provides a "cushion" for wet snow while the blue provides a grip for the powder snow. This particular combination can work for breakable crust conditions or for a light layer of powder snow on top of a crust. Cushions are sometimes applied with hard waxes, such as red covered by *Swix* blue. These are some suggestions, but generally the transition snow conditions can be very frustrating.

• Backcountry skiers seldom cork skis unless they are in transition snow conditions where the ski may be sticking too much. Often, with fiberglass skis I will use the next softer wax than the waxing chart shown here indicates to provide better grip.

• Klisters are made for applying in warm rooms or klister huts. Since these aren't found along the trail, the two-wax system is commonly used. Waxes such as *Jack Rabbit Wet* and *Toko Plus* are made for klister conditions and can be applied like a crayon on the ski in the same way as a hard wax. Klister tubes have to be heated to apply the klister. You can use several methods to heat the tube: 1) put the tube in a warm pants pocket while you're skiing; 2) put the tube between your legs or under armpits—be sure the tube doesn't leak; 3) hold the tube over a candle that can be placed behind a pack used as a wind break; 4) set the klister tube in the sun; and, 5) fire up the stove and warm the tube over it. The last is the best method. When the klister is warm and it will flow easily, apply it to the ski quickly. The klister will cool rapidly once it is away from the heat source.

• In the spring, klisters can pick up dirt and pine needles, and lose their grip on the snow. Then it becomes necessary to scrape the ski and apply new klister. Silver klister can be added to help keep other klisters cleaner. For mushy conditions, *Rode* klisters are excellent.

Removing Wax

Transitional Snow

You can carry special liquid wax removers for day trips; but, on overnight trips, wax removers are extra weight. White gas can be used. The following method may not be endorsed by racing coaches, but it does remove klister and other wax quickly: *Step one*—lay skis down on the snow with the bottoms up. *Step two*—sprinkle white gas over the entire bottom. This is where a fuel bottle with a small hole in the cap comes in handy. *Step three*—let skis sit for approximately 20 to 30 seconds. *Step four*—scrape off wax with a scraper and finish wiping it off with the small rag carried in your wax kit. If some wax remains, use a little more gas.

Sooner or later a backcountry skier will have to deal with that terrible stuff known as transitional snow. Waxing is difficult and most of the time no wax works. There are some techniques that help:

- Find a wax that gives you some grip. If it is on the fringe of balling up and collecting clumps of snow under the skis, keep sliding the skis. Avoid making steps with the skis (lifting the ski and setting it down) because this forces the snow into the wax and causes balling.
- If the skis start to ball up, give them a whack with your pole to knock the snow off; then go back to the sliding motion. Be careful. You can break both fiberglass and cane poles this way.
- Another method of cleaning snow off the bottom of your skis is to roll your ankle, turning one ski on its side. Scrape the other ski back and forth against the edge of the ski on its side. When that ski is clean, reverse the process.
- If the skis are sticking too much and driving you bananas, scrape the wax off until sticking is solved. You can use a little gas from the stove to really clean them off. You may have to use a harder wax, and if that slips, you'll have to do more poling and herringbone.

SKIING TECHNIQUES

Skiing took a turn in the early 1900's. By then, although the miners and winter travelers of the western mountains were still using skis, the pitch of the ski fever of the late 1800's had subsided. The emphasis changed to the eastern U.S. and Canada where big strides were being made. Improved equipment was becoming available and skiers were putting it to good use. The famous Canadian cross-country skier, Herman "Jackrabbit" Smith-Johansen, set up an 80-mile backcountry touring route in the Laurentian Mountains. He would often ski the route in four days carrying his heavy pack, an axe, and with his dog trailing along behind. The telemark turn was going strong on the open slopes along Jackrabbit Maple Leaf Trail and in the hardwood forests of the East.

Eventually cross-country skiing and Alpine skiing evolved into two different sports as lifts were developed in the mid-

1930's and proliferated in years following. Equipment became more specialized. With most of the emphasis on Alpine skiing, the telemark turn was almost forgotten except for a few old-timers who knew a good turn and were quietly executing telemarks on nearby slopes.

Jackrabbit was one of those old-timers. He loved exploring and skiing the nearby hills and mountains under his own power. In a 1975 *Nordic World* article commemorating his 100th birthday, he told skiers how much they were missing by limiting their experience to ski areas where "you never see anything but the points of your skis."

When cross-country skiing began to catch on in the late 60's and early 70's, the telemark was revived. For many of the new skiers, climbing to the top of a hill to link telemarks became the essence of skiing.

Telemark turns don't begin until the top of the hill, so let's start climbing first.

UPHILL TECHNIQUES

If the hill isn't too steep, you can just plod to the top. When the wax begins to slip, stamp down the ski, making a pronounced step-like motion instead of a sliding motion. This will push the wax into the snow to create a better grip. When you feel a slip, sometimes it will help to roll the ankle and edge the ski. If the hill is short, stamping and using the edges might be enough.

If your group is in single file on a broken trail and the wax begins to lose its grip, you can step one or both skis on to the soft snow off the trail to obtain a better grip. These techniques are fine for a short stretch, but they get tiring over the long haul.

Arnor Larson

Uphill Traverse   Herringbone

If skiing straight up becomes tiring, traverse the hill by veering off to a more gradual angle. If you slip on the traverse, try stepping the heels of your skis a little uphill with each step. You might also try angling your downside ski downward to form a half herringbone for more grip.

Stepping up heels on an uphill traverse.

For more holding power to climb uphill, use the herringbone by forming a "V" with your skis, with the tails of the skis at the point or apex of the "V". The skis are planted behind you and are used as support, as you alternately pick up each ski, keeping the skis angled out. To keep from slipping, set the inside edges into the snow with each step.

The tracks create a herringbone pattern that gives the technique its name. It is tiring with a pack, however, and is usually used only for short climbs, or for quick holding power to keep from toppling over. It's good for changing direction on a slope.

Herringbone.

Fletcher Manley

Side Step

Traverse Side Step

The side step is used for short, steep pitches, and is easier than the herringbone in deep snow conditions. It is made by putting the skis perpendicular to the slope and stepping uphill, keeping the skis parallel. The ski is lifted and controlled by the toe. In loose snow, you'll need to free the ski by kicking it forward to get the tip on top of the snow, then pulling up to free the tail. The side step is very helpful when you are confined to a narrow passageway.

Also called a forward side step, this is simply a side step and traverse done at the same time. As you step up with the uphill ski, advance it forward a foot or so, then bring the downhill ski up to the uphill ski, and continue across and up the hill, gaining altitude with each step. The traverse side step is convenient for climbing short, steep, open patches in trees where the traverse/kick turn technique described next would demand many tiring, short traverses and kick turns.

Traverse
Kick Turn

This is, by far, the most common way of climbing a hill. Start by skiing straight up the hill until the wax starts slipping. Then turn and traverse the hill at a comfortable angle. Continue the switchback by traversing the hill, stopping, getting your skis level, making a kick turn, and continuing the traverse in a new direction.

Kick turns ordinarily are made by kicking the downhill ski around first which is certainly the best type to use on steep pitches. Another turn involves kicking the uphill ski around first. On some pitches, this feels more comfortable and gives you some relief from doing a regular kick turn all the time.

Keep traverses at a comfortable angle. If you are traversing too steeply, the skier following you may be slipping since your wax will have a better grip in the softer, untracked snow. Try to keep kick turns to a minimum. It's tiring to do kick turns one after another.

Below: *kick turn sequence.*

Skins or Climbers

Skins and rope climbers can be an asset for long climbs on a backcountry trip. Skins can climb at a remarkable angle. Once in the San Juans in Colorado, I was climbing with a group to the top of an avalanche path to take some measurements in the fracture zone. Terry Young of the Trucker Ski Company was using skins.

As we ascended the path, we took slope angle measurements with a clinometer. At one point, he was skiing straight up a slope at almost a 30-degree angle—a steep slope indeed. When he hit the 30-degree range, he toppled over.

If you don't have any skins or rope climbers, a few loops of 3/8"-1/2" rope around the ski will give additional holding power when you are having waxing trouble. Clip it under the binding bail to keep it in place.

Coming Back Down

DOWNHILL TECHNIQUES

Skiing downhill, Nordic style, is a subject that fills books. I will emphasize the important basic points relating to backcountry skiing. If you know the basics, the fine points will follow.

There are a few general points which apply to all downhill techniques. The most important is to stay soft and flexible in the knees so you can absorb terrain changes. Keep your hands out in front of your body in your field of vision, and use them to help keep your balance.

On a day tour, when the pack on your back is light, you will be able to do much more downhill skiing. A heavy pack restricts downhill technique. You're going more slowly with more control and can't do a lot of fancy turns. Conservative skiing is the norm for backcountry and you make up for it by seeing more and different terrain over a longer period. Never go to the backcountry thinking that someone will come to the rescue if you are injured. One of the good things about being in the backcountry is that we have to take responsibility for our actions. The backcountry teaches you how to handle your own problems.

Various downhill Nordic techniques are pictured and discussed here. Use the techniques with which you feel the most comfortable. When I'm skiing in the backcountry with a heavy pack, I use the traverse/kick turn the most, step turns on gradual slopes, snow plow turns, sometimes the stem, and a little bit of the telemark in deep, soft snow. They are all simple, reliable turns that have taken me safely across miles and miles of winter wilderness.

Straight Down

Traverse Kick Turn

If the hill isn't too steep, and your descent path looks safe, skiing straight down may be the way to go. The position, called the straight running position, is relaxed. Knees are soft. Hands are in the field of vision, and one ski is slightly advanced.

The traverse kick turn is simply the downhill version of the uphill technique discussed before. Traverse down the slope at a comfortable angle. While traversing, keep your skis approximately at shoulder width apart for stability. Most of your weight is placed on the downhill ski. The uphill ski can be used to control speed by weighting and pushing it into the softer, untracked snow. Knees should be bent slightly and flexible. Step the ski slightly uphill to slow down and stop. Then do a kick turn and traverse again. This is the most common method of descending a hill. It is the safest since you can make shallow traverses and keep speed to a minimum. When I'm alone, I do a lot of these.

Traverse kick turn.

Snowplow

The snowplow is usually the first turn a skier learns. The snowplow is a good turn to use on gradual slopes with a good base, on slopes with a light surface layer of snow, in spring corn, and occasionally in breakable crust. Remember to keep the skis edged by rolling the ankle inward and pushing heels out in a wedge to control speed. *Loipus* heel locators are an asset for snowplowing with a pack. Upper body is erect, arms should be held to the side, hands out in front, and poles back. Keep the knees flexible.

Left and below: *snowplow. The woman on the left in the picture below has her hands too far back.*

Step Turn

Step turns are commonly used on gradual slopes for changing direction. Sometimes a step turn will help when the snow is heavy and resists other turns. The step turn is carried out by stepping the tips of the skis in a new direction. Pick up the tip of the downhill ski, pulling the ski clear of the snow and point it in the direction of the turn. Then pick up the other ski and bring it close to the first ski.

Continue these little steps until the turn is complete. As in any turn, the upper body should be relaxed. Squat slightly as you step. Try to minimize upper body movement. Quite often, turns on gradual slopes involve stepping in one direction to get around an obstruction such as a tree, then stepping in the other direction and so on down the slope.

Step turn.

Stem Turn

The stem turn is another convenient turn which you can use on a packed surface or on a good base with a thin surface layer of snow. Traverse the slope, step uphill with the tail of the ski (called stemming) into a snowplow. Make a snowplow turn. As soon as you have nearly completed the turn, and are faced in the new direction, let the skis run parallel together. Traverse the slope and repeat the stem. Keep your knees flexible and skis shoulder width apart for stability. There are more variations of the stem turn, but this is the most common style for the backcountry situation.

Stem turn.

Telemark Turn

The telemark is a beautiful, flowing turn. When the sun is out, the powder light and deep, there isn't anything in the realm of skiing that compares to the elegance and grace of linking a series of telemark turns down a slope.

Here are some steps to help you learn the telemark:

- Start by learning the basic position on flat ground. Plant your poles next to you, then drop down in the telemark position by advancing one ski. Think in terms of your knees. The knee of the leading leg should be positioned over the ball of the leading foot. The knee of the trailing leg is positioned directly below the hip. Commonly the skis are positioned so the tip of the rear ski is next to the boot of the lead ski. If you have a heavy pack, then the telemark position is much more upright. Hold that position for a moment, then switch legs, advancing the other ski forward. This is a good warming up exercise.

Below and right:
telemark turn.

- Start learning the turn by practicing near the bottom of a hill. Climb up the hill several meters and ski straight down. At the bottom, where the hill levels out, try a telemark turn to one side. For a right turn, drive the left knee (remember to think in terms of knees) in the direction of the turn as you drop into the telemark position. When the turn is completed, rise up, bringing the skis back together again. Do this for both sides until it feels comfortable.

- If you can execute telemarks at the bottom of the hill, linking them on a slope will soon follow. The essential point to remember about linking telemarks is that, after you've made one, come back up to the traverse position. If necessary, gain stability by using a wide stance. Then drop back into the next telemark, make the turn, come up, and drop back down again in a smooth and rhythmic motion.

Parallel Turn

The parallel turn can be learned by progressing beyond the stem turn. It is achieved by using less and less of a stem to initiate the turn, and more of a twist of both skis in the desired direction. The twist, a driving knee motion in the direction of the turn, occurs while you unweight the skis by sinking, then rising up.
The skis are kept wide apart for balance and stability - not close together. As the skis are weighted, there is a definite setting of the edges. The other important aspect of the turn is to keep shoulders facing down the slope. As turns are made to one side, the body should be twisted for a moment with shoulders facing downhill and legs in the direction of the turn. Then, as you unweight, the upper and lower body uncoils, helping execute the next turn. The poles come into play, helping to establish rhythm and to initiate turns.

Parallel turn.

Through Trees

Certain precautions should be taken while skiing through trees. The most important measure is to take your hands out of the pole straps. Pole baskets can get caught in branches and pull you off balance, or even dislocate a shoulder. It happened to me once, descending a near-by mountain. Fortunately, my shoulder snapped back in place and ever since I've always kept my hands out of the straps.

Skiers don't use the pole straps for any downhill skiing. A quick way of safely positioning your hand is to pull your thumb out of the strap and regrasp the handle, leaving only the fingers of your hand still in the strap. Wear sunglasses or goggles to protect your eyes from poking branches. Be careful not to fall into tree wells which are big depressions that form around large trees.

Keep the thumb outside the strap when skiing through trees.

The
Unexpected   Falling

Ice is bad stuff no matter how you scrape across it. On ice, it is necessary to exaggerate edging the skis into the slope, putting most of the weight on the downhill ski. For stability, use a wider stance. On gradual slopes, it may be possible to snowplow. On steeper slopes, try side-slipping by releasing your edges and allowing the ski to slip sideways down the hill. Skins are very helpful.

When encountering dips, bumps, or skiing from a slick snow surface such as crust to slower snow such as powder, drop into a telemark position. The position will provide forward and backward stability and balance.

There's no fancy downhill technique for breakable crust. The most common means of descending on breakable crust is to make a gradual traverse across the slope. When the crust breaks and causes a fall, try to fall uphill into a sitting position. The descent is continued by making more traverses and falling into the sitting position whenever the crust throws you off balance. Not exactly the most graceful form, but at least it's functional.

It's going to happen and the big pack on your back complicates matters. Watch out for external frame packs which can bang you on the back of the head. It's a good idea to put some padding there.

When you feel the fall coming, relax. Don't straighten arms stiffly to take the impact of the fall. Stiff, tense muscles are more susceptible to injury than relaxed, pliable muscles. Try to sit down and fall to the side. Avoid head-first falls.

Sometimes you can squirm your way back up to a standing position. More often, you'll have to release your waist belt. This is when a quick release buckle is very handy. Slide the pack off. Stand up and brush off the snow. If you're on a hill, step downhill so your pack is uphill from you. Skis should be parallel, wide apart and perpendicular to the fall line. Lift the pack onto one knee, then from the knee up to the shoulders.

Slowing Down

A common situation is skiing down narrow trails, roads, and snowmobile tracks with trees on either side. Controlling your speed is difficult in these situations since you can't traverse back and forth and make kick turns. Often the narrow trails are iced and rutted. Here are a few procedures that might help:

- Sometimes, on gradually-sloped trails, you can create enough of a drag to slow down by edging the ski. This can't be used for a very long way but it may be enough to lead into another technique.

- When you are going slowly try to snowplow. With a rutted trail, it may be difficult to hold this position. If you need to stop quickly, such as at the edge of a stream or just before a log across the trail, a ski pole check can be used. The check is made by planting the poles in front of you, and trying to stop abruptly by using the poles to take the impact of your forward motion. Some of the shock can be absorbed in the arms. Be careful with this one. Keep your arms well to the sides since they can jam into your chest if your momentum continues. If your speed is too great, you may injure yourself by using a pole check.

Above and right: *pole drags are a sure way to slow down.*

101

- If the snow is soft on one side of the packed trail, you can ski into the softer, more resistant snow to slow down.
- Use the old-timers' pole drag. They put their one pole between their legs and sat on it to slow down. Use both poles. Take your hands out of the straps and put the two poles together There are various ways of holding the poles. I put one hand in front of my legs and one in back to support the poles and to prevent breakage. The disadvantage is that it's hard to get in this position while wearing a heavy pack, and it can bend or break poles.
- One of the most useful pole drags was shown to me by Sandy Gebhards, who comes from a back-country skiing family. In this technique, grab each pole, palms up, one-third of the way down from the handle, pointing the baskets away from you. Put the handles under your armpits and hold your arms very tight against the poles and your side as you slide down the hill. This is a good technique for steep roads.

- The most effective method of slowing down on steep, narrow trails is by using skins or rope climbers. You can also slip a few loops of rope over the ski. This is a jerky method of descending, and you will have to use the telemark position often to keep your balance.
- You can always walk down, which sometimes is the most efficient technique.

A pole check is a good stop when you're already going slow.

Staying in Touch

Heavy Packs

Downhill skiing is one of the easiest times to get separated from a group. You should stick together as you're descending. If someone has an accident 1,000 feet above you, it's a long climb back.

Downhill skiing provides some of the most enjoyable experiences of the trip. It's a time to watch some dramatic falls, to cheer on your mates and to reap the rewards of those long climbs.

Turns can't be as fancy with a pack on your back. Comparing backcountry downhill to Alpine downhill at a ski area is like comparing walking through a meadow and dodging across a Manhattan street. Backcountry is an aspect of skiing where little things mean a lot. Linking four or five turns with a heavy pack may be the highlight of a whole week's trip.

CAMPING & COOKING

One of the most interesting campsites I've ever experienced was set up unexpectedly after seven days of a trip into the snow-shrouded Crags in the midst of primitive wilderness. Four of us were approaching a critical point in our traverse. The one pass we were looking for was a low saddle between higher and more rugged peaks. It was the only way to cross the backbone of the range and reach the other side of the divide.

Snow swirled as we gathered around the map. We couldn't see any landmarks, yet we were anxious to keep moving. We were convinced that the slope ahead of us was the right direction and we continued climbing higher and higher.

After an afternoon of climbing, we reached the top of the ridge. If we had made the right choice, it would be an easy ski to the pass. We dropped our packs and skied to the edge, only to peer over an abrupt cliff that fell a thousand feet to disappear mysteriously in the clouds.

Obviously the wrong choice. After the clouds cleared enough we could see our objective a half mile to the north across the basin. Although it was somewhat unsettling to know we would have to make an unplanned camp on an exposed ridge, it turned out to be the most spectacular winter camp I've ever made. Eventually, the clouds began to lift. Through the opening of our tent high on the ridge, we watched the framed moving picture of clouds billowing and tumbling, now covering, then breaking dramatically to unveil snow-burdened peaks.

Although high, exposed ridges can be dangerous during bad weather, they're also one of the most scenic locations for a winter campsite.

Selecting a Campsite

When the weather looks kind, a camp in a high location overlooking the surrounding scenery can make a trip. You are out there for enjoyment and beautiful scenery and views should certainly be one consideration when choosing a campsite. Other concerns are:

Wind protection. Trees, outcroppings, and a large pine all provide protection from wind. Watch for loaded branches of snow, and place the tent so that you are not directly under them.

Avalanche hazard. Avoid camping on any slope or at the bottom of any slope that would have the remote possibility to avalanche. Learn to check the surroundings for vulnerability below open areas, steep, narrow chutes or overhanging cornices. It is always important to learn the telltale signs of avalanche conditions.

Water availability. This is especially important. Having a source of water from an open stream saves a lot of fuel and time melting snow. Often, however, the streams are frozen or covered by snow. On a trek through a wilderness area, one group had running streams at only two of the ten campsites.

Altitude. Avoid valley bottoms and low meadows. Cold air will settle in lower areas and make a chilly, frosty camp.

Putting up the Tent

You are probably used to setting up your tent, but there are conditions peculiar to winter camping.

- Stamp out a level platform with your skis on, and use them to compact the snow. You can compact it further by stamping it out with your boots, but it isn't necessary. You can make it level by shoveling out a platform.
- Place the entrance downhill. Cold air will flow into a tent facing uphill. Place the tent ninety degrees to the wind.
- With your skis on, stake out the tent. If you have a dome or tunnel tent, put the poles in place and then stake it out. Throw everyone's pad inside. Then, as you slip into the tent, the pads will cushion you and prevent pits in the snow under the tent. After some time, the snow firms up and provides a platform to sleep on. An unjustified fear of those first trying winter camping is that the snow will melt on contact with the tent, bodies or bag. That doesn't happen.
- Skis and ski poles can be used for tent stakes if you've elected not to bring any snow stakes with you.
- In front of the tent door, dig a square hole one to two feet deep. This will serve as a porch when brushing off boots or changing socks.

Benches and platforms above the meadow or valley will be warmer.

Terrain. The easiest location for a tent is obviously a flat area but, if not available, simply make a platform by using the shovels and digging out a place in the snow. This is one of the luxuries of winter camping: snow can be moved.

Once a site has been selected, the members of the group should divide up the tasks of setting up camp, putting up tents and making a kitchen area. The temptation might be there to sit and relax but it's important to get the heavy work over with while still warm and energized. Work has the attractive advantage of keeping you warm.

Kitchen

While some are setting up the tent, others can be constructing the kitchen. If it is bitter cold, then you may dispense with the kitchen and do all the cooking in the tent while wrapped in sleeping bags. In most winter weather, however, cooking can be done outside. After one too many spilled cups of soup on my sleeping bag, I avoid tent cooking whenever possible.

The kitchen area can vary in size depending on how much time you have and how energetic you feel after skiing all day. Ideal kitchen areas are three to four feet deep rectangular holes shoveled in the snow. The length should be five to eight feet and the width three to four feet. A shelf should be made in the snow approximately one foot below the top of the hole where a stove can be set and all cooking is done. If you are tired, a kitchen may consist of a small hole deep enough to stand in and to keep the stove out of the wind.

The nice thing about such kitchens is their convenience. If deep enough, you can work with the stove and do all of the cooking without bending or kneeling. The essential factor is that the stove is

protected from the wind. Like kitchens at home, they're places where everyone from the party congregates and chats about the day's activities.

The most ambitious kitchen I've ever seen was about eight feet deep and covered with a tarp. It had shelves, a cooking area, and storage.

When the kitchen is constructed, get the stove out, fill it up, and start melting water right away. A small ensolite pad placed under the stove will help insulate it from the snow and keep it working more efficiently.

Changing Clothes

Cooking

While setting up the tent and constructing the kitchen, you'll be working and keeping warm. But, sometime after those chores, the activity level drops and you'll need to be careful to put on dry, warmer clothing *before* you chill. Most skiers change into a dry pair of socks and then pull on a pair of down or fiberfill booties. Over the booties, a pair of water-resistant overboots can be worn for walking around in the snow. The bootie-overboot combination does the trick when it comes to keeping warm while standing around in camp. It feels good to get out of ski boots.

By the time members of the group have changed into warmer clothing and laid out sleeping bags in the tent, the water on the stove is likely to be hot. First on the program is a hot drink for everyone. Cocoa, tea, hot jello—whatever everyone enjoys. The idea is to start replacing lost fluids right away and at the same time to provide extra heat to the body.

You should consume at least a gallon of water each day. Often skiers only get a quart of water during the day from their water bottles if no open streams are available. That means another three quarts will have to be consumed at breakfast and supper. Be aware of this quantity because being thirsty isn't always a reliable indicator of being dehydrated. Dehydration can lead to fatigue, contributes to making you colder, and can lead to hypothermia. Drink water whenever you can and be conscious of your daily water intake. I try to keep drinking liquids to the point of forcing it.

For the main course, cooking will be easy since you've taken care of all the preparation before leaving on the trip. Freeze-dried foods are simply dropped into the hot water and allowed to soak for a few minutes. If you are preparing one pot meals with grocery store ingredients, all the mixing and combining of ingredients has been done at home. All you need to do is to add it to a pot. Put spoonfuls of butter or margarine on the food to raise its caloric value.

When supper is finished, keep the stove going for more hot drinks.

Pollution

Stove Safety

Winter is as necessary a time as any to minimize environmental impact. Vegetation that can be trampled and destroyed at summer campsites is well protected under a layer of snow. The problem of winter camping is human waste. One characteristic of freeze-dried food is that it keeps you regular. The winter camper should take care to find a bathroom site well away from any streams or drainage paths. If winter campers are careless, the spring melt will wash all the preserved human waste from the winter into the streams during a short period of time, fouling the stream early in the season.

Pick up litter. Don't be conned into believing that the protective white blanket will miraculously sweep away any litter. Particularly be careful not to drop wax wrappers. If you bring oranges, carry out the peels. Pine boughs should only be used for emergency shelters.

An abandoned campsite not properly cleaned up can look quite ugly in these white surroundings especially if another party happens along within the next few days. Out of courtesy, I throw snow over urine marks and food spills before leaving. I have skied by winter camps that were filthy. At one camp left by a large, commercial "winter survival" school, a companion found unused tea bags and a dollar bill.

Stoves are dangerous if handled improperly. If possible, cook outside the tent to be safe. It is not always possible, and some cooking probably will have to take place in the tents. It may be feasible to set the stove just outside the tent door.

Whatever you do, treat it with caution. Stoves produce carbon monoxide. Try to do any fuel filling out in the open.

A few points to remember:

- Solid fuel or fire starter pellets are the safest primer for stoves, especially when cooking in tents. White gas used as a primer flares up violently while solid fuel burns predictably.

- Avoid wrapping the stove in any kind of insulation. Use only insulation under the base of the stove.

- If the tank becomes so hot it can't be touched, turn off the stove and let it cool.

- Most stoves have a safety release valve in the cap. If too much pressure builds up in the stove, gas will escape out of the safety release. Usually the escaping gas will ignite throwing flame away from the stove. Keep the cap pointed away from you and outside the tent door.

- Fill the tank before starting to cook. If you have to fill the tank while cooking, allow it to cool off before fueling. A funnel is a considerable help in filling.

- Gas can assume the air temperature and can cause frostbite if spilled on hands during subzero days.

Water

- After filling, replace the cap on the fuel bottle and place it far away from where you are operating the stove.
- Because stoves produce carbon monoxide gas, always make sure your tent, snow cave, or igloo is well ventilated.

In the winter when water surrounds you, it's surprising to be worried about it. Yet, making sure you have enough of it is a constant concern. If you're in an area where open streams or lakes exist, you'll have a ready supply. Often, however, you'll find that all water has to be melted. It takes time and fuel to melt snow, but avoiding fatigue, headaches, and eventually dehydration is worth it.

Melted snow water in a pot never tastes as good as from a mountain brook. You can help its taste and speed up the melting process by pouring a bit of water left over from a water bottle in the bottom of the pan. Allow it to warm and add snow, just enough that the snow doesn't soak up all the water. If you're cooking inside your tent, pile up bits and chunks of snow just outside the entrance, in order to have your snow supply within reach. Bring plenty of juice mixes, cocoa, coffee or tea to help disguise the pan taste.

Getting Settled

To make your sleeping area more comfortable, position yourself in a desired location, then bounce up and down jamming your buttocks into the pad, making a depression for your hips. This will help keep the pad in position as well as being more comfortable for sleeping.

To avoid confusion and accidents, it is best for tent mates to get in the tent separately. Brush snow off clothing. Boots can be removed while sitting in the tent and hanging your legs over the porch.

Knock snow off the boots before bringing them in so the tent doesn't get wet.

A candle can be tied to a tent's center pole or set on a pot. Some skiers bring small candle lanterns to hang in the tent when arranging and sorting equipment. I like to write in my notebook before retiring at night and a candle gives enough light.

Keeping Warm

Those who have never tried winter camping may have steered clear of it for fear of freezing during the night. It's an understandable concern, but unjustified. With a few simple precautions, no one is going to be found a frozen zombie the next morning. While the proper sleeping bag will keep you from freezing, here are some helpful hints for staying comfortably warm:

- The important first step is to get into the sleeping bag warm. Don't expect the sleeping bag to warm you. It can, but you'll be ahead of the game if you are warm when you first climb into the bag. If you're not warm, drink lots of hot liquids or go for a quick ski to get the blood circulating.

Inside a snow cave.

- Eating something right before you hit the sack can help. It also gets the blood circulating for the digestive process and provides a little extra energy.

- Keep sleeping bags close together in the tent. Take advantage of some of your partner's heat.

- Wearing clothing inside the sleeping bag is the most important aid to increasing your comfort at night. If you're not warm enough, put on a hat. Wear shirts and jackets if you are still chilly. Still more warmth can be obtained by wearing down booties and mittens.

- Keep the bag's hood closed up, leaving only a small opening for your mouth. The hood drawn up in this way helps to contain heat from the head and neck area.

- If you're still cold, get more insulation under your body by placing your pack under the pad and any left over clothing under your bag.

- If you happen to be sleeping outside and not in a tent, stay warmer by finding a protected location out of the wind. Sleep under cover such as under branches or build a snow shelter (see end of this chapter).

- If you're still cold, think about getting a new bag and thicker pad. Some of us have systems that simply can not handle colder temperatures as well as others.

- If you become very cold, don't be afraid to wake someone.

Cold Boots

Boots in bed? Some do, some don't. If you don't, you can expect stiff, frozen boots in the morning. While having them in the bag can be a little uncomfortable, those who do will have toasty boots. Place both boots in one stuff bag or each in their own bag and arrange them someplace in the sleeping bag where it's comfortable. Moist mittens and socks can be dried by placing them underneath your shirt next to your warm skin.

Gaiters commonly freeze up. Before retiring, knock the snow off and place them under your bag. Or put them in the same stuff bag as your boots and take them to bed. If you have problems with the zipper, rub on snow seal or candle wax.

Mornings

The first person awake in the morning should bravely get up and fire up the stove. He or she can get the others going by serving them hot drinks in their sleeping bags. However it is done, the first thing to do is to prepare hot drinks.

If I put the stove just outside the tent door, I can heat water in the morning without leaving the warmth of my sleeping bag.

Boots, which have been kept warm in sleeping bags all night, can be tied together and hung around your neck underneath a jacket. This will help keep them warm until you're ready to leave.

Keep drinking hot drinks after break-fast to start the day with a good supply of fluids. Even while packing, pause and sip a little cocoa, hot liquid jello or whatever.

The last thing to do after the tents are down and packs packed is to remove down booties and put on your boots. The boots will be warm from hanging underneath your jacket. Warm boots with warm feet is the *only* way to start touring. Feet are one of the hardest parts of the body to warm up. If they start to get cold, it may be a couple of miles down the trail before they again feel comfortable.

Pack overboots and down booties, check to make sure the camp is clean, and you're off for another day.

Snow Caves

Under most circumstances, snow shelters are not necessary. When it is very cold, or if the group wants to try its hand in constructing one, here are some types and tips.

Snow is a good insulator. Carefully constructed snow caves, igloos and trenches are warmer than any tent. The warmest shelter possible is a snow cave, so let's start there.

The advantage of a snow cave is its greater warmth. It can be many degrees below zero outside, but inside the cave it will be relatively toasty. After shivering through a below-zero night in a tent in the Tetons, we built a snow cave and were warm and comfortable for the second night. It may even become so warm, you'll have to make more vents to prevent melting and dripping. And a snow cave can weather the most severe winter weather imaginable. Even though the wind is howling, it will be quiet and windless inside the cave.

The disadvantage of a snow cave is that it takes time to build. Depending on its size, it can take anywhere from an hour to several hours of work while a tent can be set up in minutes. If you're traveling each day on a tour, a snow cave is usually not practical. Making a snow cave is also a wet job. Since keeping clothing dry is of vital importance in winter living, it is necessary to wear adequate water proof clothing.

You'll need at least five feet of snow to build a cave. Ideally, you'll want enough depth to stand up. Use your ski pole to check depth beforehand. If the snow isn't deep enough, it is possible to shovel snow into a huge pile for the cave, but it's a lot of work.

The ideal place to build a cave is on a hill. Look for places on the leeward side of a hill or ridge just below the top where the wind has drifted snow. Here you solve two problems: the snow is deep enough and it's on a slope. If there are no hills, a cave can be started from a tree well, but a hill is by far the most efficient.

Put on waterproof clothes and start digging. The entrance should be about four feet high and three or four feet wide. Dig straight into the hill. As you begin to dig, someone else can use another shovel and keep moving away the debris. Working

Snow cave entrance.

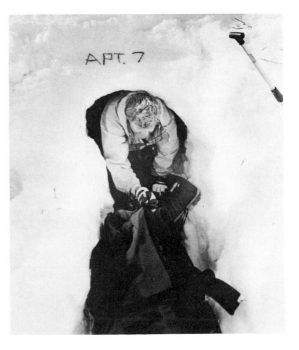

on a hill makes this easier because the debris can be thrown downhill.

As digging progresses, start slanting the entrance tunnel slightly upward. This will make it easy to slide snow out and will also allow cold air to flow out of the cave. In any kind of snow structure, always make entrances lower to keep out cold air. Dig straight back several feet and then start widening the cave, digging upward if you have enough snow depth so it will be

Carve a domed ceiling in the snow cave.

possible to stand. Switch off digging with other members of the party to avoid exhaustion and to do the job quickly. Once you are into the cave, dig a sleeping platform. The platform ideally should be above waist level or at the same level as the top of the entrance.

The top of the cave should be shaved into a dome shape. The dome provides structural strength to the cave. Keep at least a one to two foot thickness of snow on the roof for adequate insulation.

Additional rooms can be connected to the cave by digging an archway much like the entrance and then by digging another cave with more sleeping platforms. Snow caves can begin to take on the appearance of a hotel with connecting rooms. I've been with groups out for a weekend when we built a snow cave system which housed 25-30 people.

The above description is an ideal situation but often you may not have ideal conditions. The snow, for example, may not be deep enough to stand in the cave. You may be digging and run into a rock or bare ground. You'll have to make adjustments and design the cave as you dig to fit its limitations.

Smooth the ceiling as much as possible to prevent water from dripping. A special place can be made for the stove. Directly above it, make a vent hole with a ski pole. Other vent holes can be made, remembering that ventilation is extremely important when using stoves.

Mark the cave with skis or poles, and bring a shovel inside. Light a candle and the cave becomes a beautiful, glowing home in the snow.

Igloos

Measuring the base diameter of an igloo.

For igloos, you'll need packed, consolidated snow. It is possible to make an igloo in powder snow by packing it thoroughly, but it does require a lot of extra work. You'll need a snow saw, which is an aluminum blade with large teeth and a handle.

Igloos take a little more skill to build than snow caves. Cutting blocks and positioning them, though not hard, takes practice. It's good not to depend on this type of shelter until you've made a few and feel confident. Igloos aren't as wet as snow caves but mittens can get wet so be sure to wear overmittens along with water-proofed clothing. One advantage of igloos is that they can be built in a snow pack with a depth of only a couple of feet. The last igloo I built was in snow 19 to 24 inches deep.

Igloos can be built on the flat or on a slope. For starters, build one on a flat area, then advance to a slope. Blocks are cut into the slope to provide building materials while leveling the floor at the same time.

Try to find the right type of snow. Look for places that have been wind drifted and packed. Sometimes under a light snow, there will be firm, consolidated snow that will work fine for igloo building. If the snow is fluffy, you can pack it down by using skis. Compact it further by stomping on it with boots. Do something else for at least a half hour to allow the snow to age, harden and become firm. As you can guess, this method is time consuming.

Draw the outline of the igloo in the snow. You can use a ski pole or ski. Set it down, hold it at a fixed point, and trace a circle in the snow. Make the circle about six to seven feet in diameter. It is at this point that many first timers fail. Too large a diameter often results in a collapsed igloo. The circle will look small, but as you cut blocks deeper in the snow, the igloo can be widened for more room.

- Start where the entrance tunnel of the igloo will be located. Dig a trench for the entrance that will be lower than the first layer of block. Dig a hole with a shovel and level the surface of one side of the hole. The first block will come from this flat side. If the snow is deep enough, cut the

blocks vertically into the snow. This will be much easier and more efficient than cutting a block in a new area each time. Sometimes, it will be necessary to go to other areas because of inadequate snow depth or a weak layer in the snow. Cut blocks as big as you can handle and carry. They should be about five to seven inches thick, around eighteen to twenty inches wide, and about two feet long.

- Cut blocks from inside the igloo circle. Span the entrance tunnel with one block and continue all around

Igloo blocks should touch at three points as they're put up.

the traced circle with the first row of blocks. Start leaning the first row toward the center of the igloo.

- Structural strength in an igloo is based on three points of contact between adjacent snow blocks. Two of the points on opposite corners provide strength; the third point keeps the block from rotating. Shave concave edges on the sides of the blocks where they meet so that when you lean and set the blocks together, they contact each other only in three points at the corners. The fourth cor-

ner of the four-cornered block will serve as the contact point for the next adjacent block.

- After the first row is laid, make a tapered cut around the circle to provide a base on which the second row of blocks can spiral upward and inward. This will produce a snail-like incline along succeeding courses that will look like a spiral ramp.
- Lay the second row of blocks. Midway through the second row, the blocks should be leaning close to forty-five degrees.

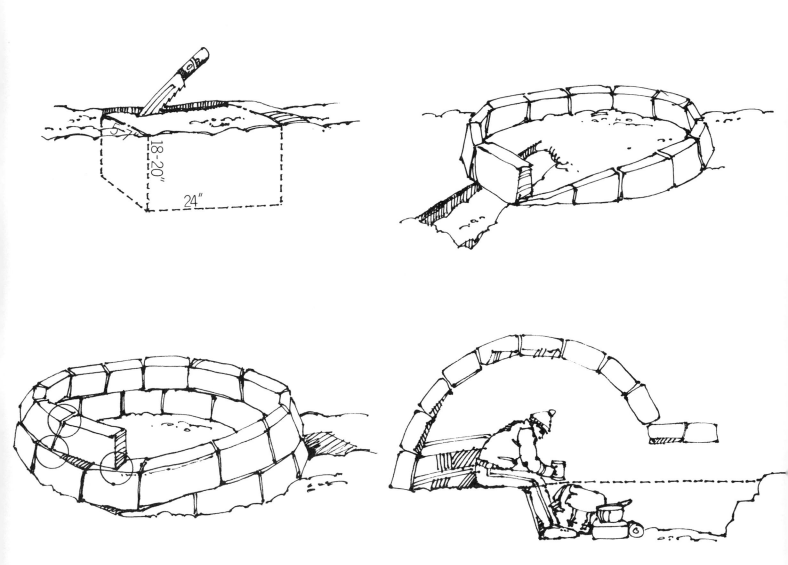

Upper left: *Cutting a snow block.* Upper right: *Tapering the first row of blocks.* Lower left: *Three points of contact.* Lower right: *Cross-section of finished igloo.*

• Continue laying blocks and constantly strive to maintain the three
points of contact. You should be able
to complete the igloo in five to seven
rows of blocks. If it takes more,
the blocks may be too small. As you
place blocks, fill in cracks with
snow. The snow will set with time,
adding more strength to the igloo.

• The igloo, like a snow cave, should
have a sleeping platform. Keep the
entrance lower than the platform to
provide a cold air sump. Platforms
can be arranged in different ways. If
you want to get fancy, the entrance
tunnel can be spanned with a block
archway.

Cutting blocks out of a snow trench.

Using blocks for an A-frame cover for a snow trench.

Snow Trenches

A snow trench is a quick, warm, one-person shelter. It is handy in an emergency situation if you happen to find yourself in the winter wilderness without shelter. It can be constructed by kicking snow out with boots and skis and removing the snow by whatever you might have available: a pot lid or just your hands. A few feet is deep enough. Dig the end of the trench deeper to serve as a cold air sump. If you have matches, a fire can be built at one end. In an emergency situation, pine boughs can serve for sleeping insulation. More pine boughs combined with sticks for support can be made into a roof.

Some skiers use snow trenches on tours for quick, warm shelters rather than sleeping in a cold tent. I made one on my last trip which I covered with skis and ski poles. The warmest snow trench is constructed by using a snow saw to cut blocks, making a trench. These blocks are set A-frame fashion over the top of the trench to form a roof. One end is sealed off and the other end can be sealed with a pack or another block.

Reading in a snow trench.

125

ROUTE FINDING

I had been sleeping beside a creek under the stars and rose early because the morning was colder than I had expected. After a quick breakfast in the bag, I continued my solo ski along a well-blazed trail through the lodgepole forest. I could see no landmarks. The rolling terrain was covered with such thick stands of timber that I was glad to have the marked trail to find my way.

The pathway of cut timber and the blaze marks on the trees made it easy to follow the route. I traveled quickly on a firm base and a light layer of cushioning snow. As the trail gradually climbed and the miles passed by, my mind drifted from one thought to another as it only can when on a solo ski trip.

Suddenly I noticed that there were no more markings. The snow was deeper and a trail was no longer distinguishable. Looking ahead I noticed a break through the trees and skied toward it. The opening was surrounded by a thick sentry of trees and I was faced with the fact that I was no longer on the trail. I retraced my tracks and looked around me, skiing in wider and wider circles hoping to pick up some sign of the trail. I found nothing. My mind began to race. Several days away from the nearest isolated ranch, I felt the first surge of panic.

I stopped, relaxed, reassured myself, and pulled out the map and compass for the first time that day. Looking at the map, I located my last night's camp and followed the dotted line indicating the trail. But where was I now? How far had I come along the trail?

I had two choices. Either I would have to retrace my tracks and this time keep alert to what streams were crossed, what directions the map showed the trail taking, and what open areas were encountered, to give me a more educated idea of the true course of the trail. Or I could try to locate a high point, climb to the top, and search for a landmark that would determine my position. The first option would consume hours and cost me the day. I decided to go with the second choice fully knowing I was at a disadvantage because I had failed to pick up bits of route information earlier in the day.

I climbed to the top of a ridge and found an open area where I could look out over the country. I set the map in the snow, oriented it, and held it in place with my ski poles. I was on a major ridge which wasn't sharp, jagged, or with rugged terrain. Though it was fairly gentle, it did divide two watersheds. All the stream valleys collected into one large stream which drained to the east in front of me. Another drainage area went off to the north behind me. Without much trouble, I located the large stream—Chamberlain Creek—on the map and identified the watershed divide on the head of the Chamberlain watershed. I was somewhere along that divide.

With that one piece of information, I was well on my way to determining my location. The divide, however, was long, and I needed to know exactly where I was before proceeding. I looked for prominent landmarks. They were scarce. All the ridges in the area were gentle hills. There were no major peaks, but there was a huge meadow in the distance. Referring again to the map, I found a large open area labeled Chamberlain Meadows. There was nothing else that could be mistaken for the large meadow.

I took a bearing on Chamberlain Meadows by lining up the engraved arrow with the compass needle. I set the compass on the map with an edge of the plastic plate on Chamberlain Meadows and turned the compass until the needle was again lined up with the engraved arrow. I placed a stick along the edge of the compass. My location was where the stick intersected the divide.

My mistakes were some of the oldest in the book: day dreaming, not paying attention, and not keeping a mental map. Route finding mistakes in the backcountry can cost you hours of time, especially in deep snow conditions that make it difficult to break trail. My troubles could have been accentuated by a heavy snowfall while I was skiing that could have covered the track behind me and caused poor visibility.

For the backcountry skier concern about route finding is an important part of the experience. The skier must recognize the risk and responsibility of venturing into the backcountry. But the risk can be controlled by knowledge of route finding techniques, a knowledge which will be invaluable wherever you go in the wilderness.

The security of being close to home is forfeited for the challenge of being able to find your way in a winter environment. This element of ski camping is a continual reminder that we are responsible for our own actions. It is only when you are out in the wilderness and have temporarily lost your bearings, that you fully recognize the importance of route finding techniques.

Arnor Larson

128

Maps

The map is a guidebook with pictures and symbols instead of words. In many instances, a map will be the sole route finding tool. It enables you to make an immediate check of your location and to continue your ski journey without fussing with a compass. A compass is important and should always be carried although most of your route finding will consist of a brief look at the map and a quick identification of surrounding features.

The most helpful maps for a skier are the Geological Survey maps which use contour lines to show the lay of the land. Maps from national, provincial and state forests, and from other land management agencies, are also helpful. These maps may be more recent than the Geological Survey maps, and will show new roads. You can see the proliferation of roads by comparing old and new maps. Our wild lands are rapidly being sliced, carved and reduced to torn fragments of once healthy wilderness. Unfortunately, we can expect more of the same in the future. If we want to continue to have roadless areas, we have to work hard through conservation groups to protect them. Thank goodness

some of our wild lands are now protected under the wilderness system. Let's keep working to protect more.

Some skiers like to cover their maps with a clear contact paper to make them more weather resistant. Others will keep their maps folded but open to the appropriate area and placed in a plastic ziplock baggie.

In the U.S., many trips require more than one 7.5 minute topo map. This is annoying when you are sighting land fea-

tures from one map to another. To avoid the problem, find out if a 15 minute map has been published which covers the area of four 7.5 minute maps. Large, 1:250,000 scale maps are available for almost any area and come in handy for sighting distant landmarks. If you know in advance that the route finding will be difficult in certain sections along the route, tape the adjacent maps together to make it easier once you are on the trail.

Map Reading

You probably have a good grasp of map techniques from other outdoor experiences. But it is important to review basic principles and to understand how they relate to backcountry skiing. Being able to read contour lines on a topographical map is essential to a skier. The following illustrations portray some of the pictures that can be formed from a map. The section of map used in the example is selected from the U.S. Geological Survey's 7.5 minute map, a map commonly used by skiers in the U.S. Elevation, shown by distances between contour lines, is indicated with each example.

In the examples below, the areas shaded grey would be shaded green on USGS maps.

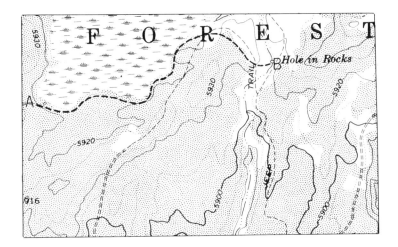

Gentle Terrain

Gentle terrain is represented by widely separated contour lines. Easy skiing, unless the terrain is covered by thick timber and/or brush.

The *shaded portions* of a contour map represent tree-covered areas. Noting the shape of open areas can help in finding your way. Using open areas is especially helpful in featureless, rolling country. For instance, a good ski route in the example from point A to "Hole in the Rock" would follow the route along the edge of the meadow as shown. (Contour interval of 20 feet.)

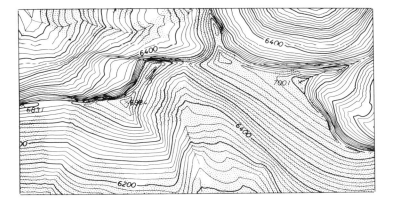

Steep Terrain

Steep terrain is represented by contour lines that are close together. Cliffs are indicated by contour lines that are very close together or on top of one another. Skiing in the area of this example is very difficult. The map shows steep, open areas which would indicate avalanche hazard. (Contour interval of 40 feet.)

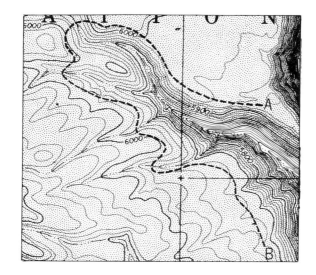

Mixed Terrain

A mixture of gentle and steep terrain is represented by some lines appearing close together and some further apart. The easiest route from point A to point B utilizes the gentle terrain as indicated by the dotted line. (Contour interval of 20 feet).

Stream valleys are represented by contour lines shaped like "V's". The apex of the "V" points upstream. The sharper the "V", the steeper the canyon.

Route finding along streams is straight forward. Simply follow the stream's course. But streams can present problems. The stream valley (which could be a canyon) in the example shown is very steep. Skiing along it would be very difficult because of the steep hillside. The bottoms of such stream valleys are deposition areas for avalanches. The best route from A to B is indicated along the rim of the canyon. (Contour interval of 20 feet.)

Ridges and Valleys

The contour lines of gentle stream valleys are shaped like "U's". The apex of the "U" points upstream. Gentle stream valleys such as the lower portion of Job Creek in this example provide easy skiing.

Though skiing may be easy in some areas, thick vegetation which often grows near a stream can make skiing difficult. Higher on the tributaries of Job Creek, the terrain becomes steeper but not overly difficult. Climbing up either of these drainages probably would require traverses and kick turns.

Between each of the tributaries of Job Creek are gentle ridges. Ridges are indicated by contour lines shaped like a "V" or "U" pointing downhill. Sharper ridges are represented by sharper "V's". The ridges shown in the example are excellent ski routes. Traveling along such ridges can often get a skier up out of the tangles of brush in stream valleys. From ridges, you can keep an eye on landmarks, have nice views, and avoid avalanche hazards. If open, however, ridges are exposed to wind and storms. (Contour interval of 40 feet.)

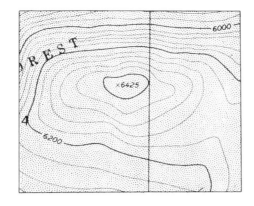

Hill or Round Point

Hills or round points are represented by wide apart, circular-shaped contour lines inside one another. The smallest, innermost circle indicates the summit. The hill in this example could be easily climbed on skis. (Contour interval of 40 feet.)

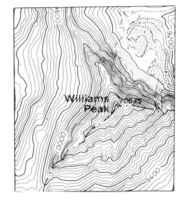

Rugged Peak

Rugged peaks are represented by closed contour lines that are very close together. The smallest inside circle indicates the top of the peak. The peak in this example has steep, precipitous slopes. Avalanche hazard is high. It may have a weakness by which it can be climbed on skis, but such an ascent is only in the realm of the experienced ski mountaineer with Alpine equipment. (Contour interval of 40 feet.)

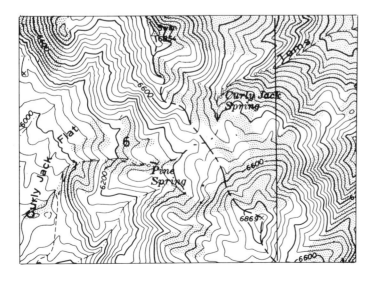

Saddle or Pass

A saddle or pass is a low point along a ridge or between two higher points where a skier can cross to the other side. The map representation of a saddle or pass is at a point where the "U" or "V" contour lines are pointed toward each other. The saddle in this example between Pine Spring and Curly Jack Spring is fairly gentle and would be a good choice for a ski route. The skiing becomes steeper downstream from Curly Jack Spring and probably requires traversing and kick turns and staying in the trees because of unstable snow conditions. (Contour interval of 40 feet.)

Compass

Compasses help to determine landmarks, to find your location and to keep you on the right course when you have no landmarks to follow. Compass bearings can be based on magnetic north or on true north. The difference between the two, known as declination, is noted on the bottom of most maps.

If you have a compass on which declination can be set, all of your readings will automatically be based on true north, once you have made the declination adjustment. With such a compass, *orient* the map by pointing true north, indicated on the bottom of your map, to the north on your compass.

If you don't have such a compass, your readings will be based on magnetic bearings. In order to use your map accurately with this type of compass, you must first *orient* your map by pointing magnetic north, indicated on the bottom of your map, to the north indicated by your compass.

Fletcher Manley

134

Landmarks

Map orientation doesn't always require a compass. You can become oriented quickly by spotting various landmarks and by turning the map so that the map lines up with surrounding landmarks. The compass, of course, is more accurate but lining up landmarks can give you a hasty reference for a routine check of your position.

Landmarks or prominent features are labeled on maps. On government survey maps, prominent features are labeled in bold letters with elevation figures while less prominent features are labeled in smaller type. When you are oriented to the map in front of you, look for the most prominent landmarks first: peaks, lakes, large meadows, major drainages. Start with the most obvious and work to the less obvious: other peaks, points, ridges, streams.

In the example, the peak and the lake are the easiest features to distinquish. A less obvious landmark, but still prominent, is the stream running out of the lake. To the right of the peak is a skyline ridge. There are two identifiable points on this ridge. A cliff just above the lake is less obvious but still worth noting for reference.

Skillful map readers are able to visualize the picture the map is making with its contour lines and symbols. They can relate this picture to their location. As you ski, the shapes of various surrounding landmarks change as you view them from different angles. You need to cultivate a feel for the appearance of terrain when viewed from different points on your map and from different directions on the trail.

Use all available clues to find routes and make it a routine to do so. For instance, let's say you have spotted the lake in the illustration from a high point. You decide it might be a nice spot to camp and start skiing to it. As you drop off the high point, the lake disappears from sight but you can still see the peak and you know the lake lies somewhere at its base. You continue skiing toward the peak. As you come closer, the top of the peak is no longer discernible. You're very close but timbered slopes prevent you from pinpointing the exact location. At this time, you can use another clue: the cliff noticed just above the lake. You catch a glimpse of the cliff through an opening in the trees and ski toward it. Soon you reach the stream which you can follow easily to the lake. If you had not made these observations from the high point, you would more than likely be floundering in the trees and wasting the time you could be using to set up camp.

Orienting Oneself

Becoming absolutely lost is a rarity these days because of the thorough mapping systems available. Except for Alaska, much of our wide expanse of wilderness is gone. When you do become disoriented, there will always be helpful information to gather. That's why it's important always to keep track of landmarks, to observe the direction you are heading, and to have an idea of how far you are traveling.

In most cases, you will need two pieces of information. This may be two landmarks that you can recognize in the distance, or one landmark and the knowledge that you are on a certain ridge, trail, or stream.

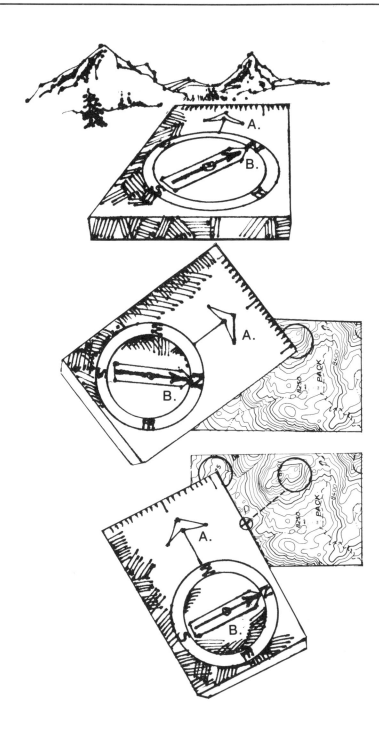

You Have Two Distant Landmarks:

The compass indicated here is the most common type with two main parts: a flat base called a protractor, and a compass dial which revolves.

Orient the map (see page 134). Take a bearing on the landmark (in this case a peak) by pointing the arrow A on the protractor at it. Turn the compass dial until the compass needle lines up within the engraved arrow B marked on the dial.

Find the landmark on the map. Don't move the compass dial. While keeping the needle lined up with the engraved arrow B, set the compass on the map with the edge of the protractor (parallel to arrow A) running through that landmark. If you have a pencil, draw a line along the edge. If not, use a pine needle or something that will mark that line. Your location is along that line.

Take a bearing on the other landmark. Repeat the process and mark another line on the map. Your location on the map is at the intersection of the two lines.

137

Have you seen these other Mountaineer Books?

Medicine for Mountaineering *Handbook for treating ills, illnesses in remote areas where no doctor is available. Compiled by climber-physicians.*

Mountains of the World *Handy guide to all major mountains and hundreds of not-so-famous peaks, by William Bueler.*

Storm and Sorrow in the High Pamirs *by Robert W. Craig. Overwhelming story of the 1974 American Pamirs Climb Expedition.*

Cascade Alpine Guide *Climbing and High Routes, by outstanding climber-author Fred Beckey. Complete climbing guides to Washington's Cascades, by Fred Beckey.*

The Ascent of Denali *First Complete Ascent of that landmark, highest Peak in North America, by Hudson Stuck, with diary of Harry Karstens.*

Snowshoeing *Complete how-to book by Gene Prater.*

Mountaineering: The Freedom of the Hills *Standard text on rock, snow, ice climbing courses of the Mountaineers. Originates on rock.*

WINTER HAZARDS

At the mention of avalanches in any of the bars in Jackson Hole, Wyoming, someone invariably tells the story of Teton Pass.

Teton Pass is located on a major East-West highway just south of Teton National Park and has a famous avalanche path known as the "Glory Slide." Some years ago, the old, winding, narrow highway was upgraded. The road was widened; curves were straightened; and much of it was replaced. One obstacle the engineers decided to take care of once and for all was Old Glory. The Glory avalanche often slides 3,000 feet as it steamrolls down the 10,000-foot Glory Mountain. The active slide path is easily visible, beginning at the huge Glory Bowl and keeping a neatly trimmed channel through the trees on the side of the mountain. At approximately 8,000 feet, the new highway dared to cross its path.

Glory slide has always been troublesome. When it slid, it covered the old highway in debris. Crews would have to clear the huge blocks of snow, sometimes closing Teton Pass for days. To prevent further problems, the engineers decided to build a bridge so Glory would slide underneath. That started the town of Jackson buzzing. Many thought it was a good idea. "Never work," some of the old-timers said.

The bridge was built and the winter before the highway was opened, every-thing seemed to go well. Then Glory slid and let loose with a whopper, baptizing the bridge with the force of a tidal wave. In a few moments, the snow bent and twisted the bridge girders. Now if you drive over Teton Pass, there's no bridge. Glory Bowl still slides, closing the pass for a while until the debris can be cleared away, just like in the old days.

Glory slide is an example of the force and power of an avalanche, but it doesn't take a big avalanche to bury a ski tourer. Most are buried in small avalanches triggered by the victims themselves. Avalanches can occur in the East as well as in the mountains of the West. Important for backcountry? Not too important if you ski on gradual, undulating terrain. But if you travel in the mountains on steep, open slopes then avalanche knowledge is critical, for it is in the backcountry where the majority of avalanche accidents occur.

Snow

Basic to understanding avalanches is knowing the different types of snow which cause them. Snow starts as ice crystals in clouds. The ice crystals grow in size until they are heavy enough to begin falling. As the snow crystal falls, it can undergo changes. One of these changes is known as riming.

In riming, the snow crystal passes through a cloud which consists of water droplets. This special type of cloud is known as a super-cooled water cloud. The water droplets are highly unstable and freeze on the snow crystals as they pass through. Some crystal shapes are completely obscured by riming, and the resulting crystal is called graupel.

Graupel, which can be observed with the naked eye, looks somewhat like a small, soft hail ball. Some skiers call it pellet snow. There are many types of crystal forms. The most common is a stellar, which is a six-sided, star-shaped crystal. Other crystals are shaped like columns, needles, plates, bullets, and a whole variety of shapes and sizes. If you are interested in the identification of snow crystals, pick up a copy of Ed LaChapelle's *Field Guide to Snow Crystals* which is an excellent guide for the skier.

Ed LaChapelle

Stellar snow crystal.

A hand lens can be carried easily in your pocket and it aids in trying to identify different snow crystals.

Once snow arrives on the ground, it begins to undergo changes. One process that occurs is called *equitemperature metamorphism*. In this process, the intricate crystals such as stellars and columns change to round grains. This process has an importance in avalanche evaluation since it tends to settle and stabilize snow packs.

If the temperature is cold and the snow pack fairly shallow, another process takes place called *temperature gradient metamorphism*. In this process, the snow crystals change to entirely different forms with sharp corners, angulated faces, layers, and sometimes a jagged cup or funnel shape. Called depth hoar, it is identified by using a hand lens and looking for sharp corners, layers, and faces. Depth hoar is normally found near the ground layers. Mechanically, this crystal is very weak. It collapses easily and is crucial to skiers since it is an important cause of avalanches.

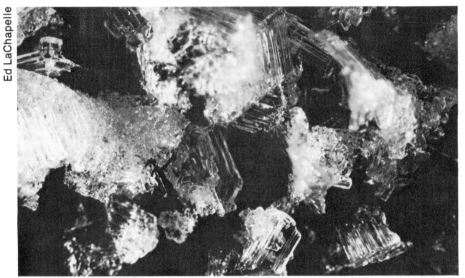

Ed LaChapelle

Right: *depth hoar crystal.*

Avalanches

There are two basic types of avalanches, depending on how they originate. If the avalanche starts from a point and spreads out, it is termed a loose-snow avalanche. If an avalanche starts from a line or fracture in the snow and begins moving as a slab or block, it is termed a slab avalanche.

Loose-snow avalanches can happen after a new, light snow falls on a slope. The new snow builds to a point when it can no longer remain on the slope, because of its weight, and then slides off. Loose-snow avalanches also may be caused by melting conditions. The water penetrates through the snow, which thus lubricated begins to slide.

Slabs beginning from a fracture line are a very dangerous form of avalanche. Many are started by victims. In a slab avalanche, an entire slab breaks loose and begins to slide. Frequently the slab lies undetected, weakly anchored to its surroundings, looming and waiting silently for a trigger to set the slab into action down the slope. A trigger can be a skier. When the trigger is provided, the release of internal tensions between the slab and its anchors may occur at lightning speed. In a split second, the entire slope may fracture into tumbling blocks.

Skiers often trigger slab avalanches.

U.S. Forest Service

Causes of Avalanches

Terrain. Steep, mountainous country is the obvious setting for avalanches. The great majority of avalanches occur on slopes with steepness between 30 and 45 degrees. Most tourers don't regularly ski slopes in this range of steepness. Watch out for small, steep sections of larger and more gradual slopes. One must also consider the slopes above where he or she may be touring. An avalanche starting on higher and steeper slopes can easily gather momentum and sweep down across the more gradual slopes where the tourer may be skiing. During periods of suspected instability, skiing is recommended only on slopes less than 30 degrees. If you are skiing in a canyon, remember that avalanches carry tremendous force and can move across valley floors with astounding speed. Skiers in many mountainous areas are familiar with that phenomenon even to the point of having seen avalanches spread across the canyon floor and start up the walls of the mountains on the other side.

The surface of the terrain has a bearing on avalanche hazard. A rough-surfaced terrain, such as that with large boulders, and brush, provides anchors for snow. As long as these anchors protrude from the surface of the snow pack and are spaced, as a rule of thumb, just close enough to make skiing somewhat annoying, the slope is likely to be safe. As they become covered, however, the succeeding layers of snow are no longer anchored and can slide.

Vegetation anchoring snow.

Other terrains, such as grassy, gravel or scree (talus or rock debris) slopes, provide smooth ground, which is a good sliding layer for an avalanche.

Trees also can provide anchoring for snow. Wooded areas generally offer "safe" routes when traveling in avalanche country. (As suggested in the Forest Service's *Avalanche Handbook*, a safe wooded area is one in which the trees are separated a few meters apart). **Sparse trees do not anchor the snow well and avalanches can, and often do, occur in wooded areas.** No route in avalanche country can be considered completely safe. Even a route in heavy timber can be hazardous if a large avalanche starts from above and tears through the timber.

The features of the terrain should guide the ski tourer in picking a safe route. Steep gullies and open slopes are natural avalanche paths. Obvious avalanche paths are plainly visible as swaths through the trees.

It is difficult, if not impossible, to understand all the factors that influence avalanche formation, but ski tourers can minimize risks by selecting safer routes of travel. The safest touring can be found in heavy timber and on ridge tops. The most dangerous traveling exists in gullies and across avalanche paths, open slopes, or at the base of steep, open slopes.

New Snow. The clearest indication of potential avalanche activity is heavy and intensive snowfall. An intensive snowfall is one in which one inch of snow falls per hour. How long these unstable conditions exist after the snow falls depends largely on temperature. Cold temperatures prolong the hazard, while warmer temperatures tend to speed up equitemperature metamorphism and its stabilizing influence.

The density of the new snow falling is also important. Dense snow crystals ac-

Arnor Larson

In the high mountains of British Columbia.

cumulating during a snowstorm can create stiff, slab avalanche conditions. Heavily rimed snow crystals, graupels, and needles, are largely the culprits and should be watched during storms.

Snowpacks. The surface of the snowpack has an effect on how well the new layers of snow will bind to it. Rough, firm, old, settled snow provides good anchoring for the new layers. Smooth, rain-crusted, sun-crusted, snowpacks provide slippery, sliding layers for new snow. Rain crusts are particularly a problem in coastal and wet snow climates.

The formation of depth hoar within the snowpack is an important consideration. Normally, skiers in wetter climates aren't

too worried about it. But it does occur when temperatures are cold and snowpacks shallow. A couple of inches of depth hoar is normal in colder, interior ranges, but five or more inches indicate a serious danger. The best way to find how much depth hoar exists in the snowpack is to dig a quick snow pit. Depth hoar crystals are mainly found on the lowest layers of the pack but can be found elsewhere.

Along with the amount of depth hoar, tourers should consider the nature of the slope. While there may be only an inch of depth hoar on a south-facing slope, a colder north-facing slope may have a foot, which would indicate unsafe touring on those north-facing slopes.

The snow pit is a very valuable tool for the backcountry tourer who is evaluating the snow's stability. Besides finding out how much depth hoar is present in the snowpack, a tourer can also get an idea of potential sliding layers. For instance, a hard, slippery crust may be located in the snowpack below a precariously perched 18 inches of consolidated snow. The 18-inch top layer of snow could very definitely form a slab avalanche. The more discontinuities a tourer observes in a snow pit, the more pronounced the avalanche hazard.

Obvious avalanche danger area.

Sometimes, when time is limited, a skier can probe the snow with his pole to get a feel of the discontinuities. It's not a very accurate test, but at least it gives the tourer more information.

Wind. Around Taberg, New York, two boys were playing on slopes along Furnace Creek one year. Strong winds and a foot of new snow created slab conditions on the leeward slopes of the creek. Both boys were caught and killed by a small avalanche. Wind is often a slab creator. Generally, winds averaging 15 miles per hour during a snowfall will form slabs on leeward sides of ridges.

Even when a long period has elapsed since the last storm, wind can create unstable conditions in a short time and under clear skies. It is obvious that the leeward sides of high ridges will have areas of wind deposition, but not so obvious are the gullies or steep, small hills in lower country. One time several years ago, a group of friends were digging a snow cave in an area of wind deposition on a short, steep hill beside a wheat field. The wind-deposited snow cracked, and several huge blocks of snow slid. Fortunately, no one was under the blocks when they slid.

Temperature. When warmer temperatures introduce melt in the snowpack, wet snow avalanches become possible. Generally, wet snow avalanches are relatively more predictable than other types. For instance, often in the spring a cold night will freeze the snowpack. Skiing on the solid snowpack the following morning will be fairly safe. This is true only after a cold night. A warm night or rain will keep wet snow avalanche danger high. As the snowpack begins to warm up during the day, free melt water begins to lubricate the snow grains, and the pack becomes unsafe. Ski when the snowpack is still frozen but be off the snow as the top layers begin to melt.

While skiing during spring conditions, tourers must observe the nature of the slope on which they are skiing. South-facing slopes will melt much faster than north slopes. It is imperative for the spring tourer to be out of the mountains or in a safe location by the time the snowpack becomes soft due to melting. It is during melting in the spring that some of the largest, most destructive wet snow avalanches occur.

Another important factor is the temperature trend during a snowstorm. If a snowfall begins warm and later cools off, then good bonding is often achieved between the old and the new snow. In the opposite situation, however, when the snowfall begins cold and then warms, poor bonding can occur and unstable conditions may result.

Travel in Avalanche Country

The safest way to travel in avalanche country is with a group of three or four. The chosen route should be planned to minimize the avalanche hazard as much as possible - stay on ridges, in thicker timber, or on windward sides of hills.

Avalanche rescue equipment should be carried. One of the best pieces of equipment that is now available for winter travel is the electronic beacon. The beacons, such as *Pieps* and *Skadis,* are small transmitters/receivers which are carried by each member of the party. If one or several members are caught in a slide, they can be located more quickly and efficiently than with any other method of rescue. Spend time with a beacon and learn how to use it efficiently.

Although avalanche beacons are being used by more and more people, Ed La-Chapelle issued a warning at a recent Mountain Hazards Symposium: "Simply wearing a *Pieps* in an avalanche doesn't guarantee any better chance of survival." LaChapelle is referring to the complacency of some skiers who think beacons are a free ticket to go and do anything, anywhere in the backcountry. There has been

greater awareness especially after a number of skiers died in avalanches wearing *Pieps*. Bringing the *Pieps* does not replace common sense, the use of good route-finding techniques, and the avoidance of travel during intensive storms.

LaChapelle continued, "We're saying that 50 percent of the victim's chances of living are up after 30 minutes, but 10 minutes is more like it and 15 minutes marginal. If you don't have the means of digging them out, you're in trouble." And,

thus, one of the most important pieces of equipment a skier can carry is a shovel. You should have a good, strong shovel that can move debris fast. Other equipment to carry includes an avalanche cord if you don't have a beacon, and ski poles which can be screwed together to form probe poles.

Before a suspected avalanche slope is crossed, the functioning electronic beacons should be stowed safely away in clothing of each of the members of the party. If no locators are available, use an avalanche cord. Remove the wrist straps of poles and safety straps of skis. Button up any clothing to prevent snow from forcing its way under clothes, then move across the suspected slope one by one. Never expose more than one person at a time in the suspected area. If one is caught, the rest of the group is then available for the rescue.

Plan the route across a suspected avalanche slope so that a quick ski run can be made to an island of safety. Islands of safety include clumps of trees, rock outcroppings, or ridges. If an avalanche starts, a skier with enough momentum may be able to reach the island before being swept away by the avalanche. The skier's momentum may also enable him to reach the flank or side of the avalanche which is usually not as treacherous as the middle.

Using a Pieps *beacon.*

Avalanche Rescue

A skier caught in an avalanche may be able to do something that will increase his chances of survival.

1. When he first realizes that he is caught, he should yell out in order that his companions can watch his descent route.

2. He should try to shed his skis, poles and pack.

3. In some cases, it may be possible to make swimming motions in an attempt to keep above the moving masses of snow. In a violent avalanche, this may not be possible.

4. Before the avalanche comes to a stop, the victim should try to bring his hand up to his mouth and nose area in an effort to create an air space for breathing.

5. He should try to thrust his other hand through the snow above him. Several avalanche victims have been quickly located because a hand was visible.

Since a buried victim's chance of survival is 50 percent after the first half hour, his likelihood of being rescued, unless help is immediately at hand, rests with his companions. These startling figures point out the need for electronic locators. If locators are not used, the rescue must proceed by more time-consuming, less accurate methods.

Avalanche probe made from two ski poles.

From the onset of the avalanche:

- The rescuers should watch carefully the path of the victim.
- Before venturing out, rescuers should check quickly to make sure other avalanches are not imminent.
- The first rescue action is to mark with a ski pole or some other item the point where the victim was last seen.
- A quick search should then be made of the area below the last seen point, looking for any more clues of the victim, such as a ski glove, pole, or pack. Mark any other items found.

- If this first hasty search fails to turn up any sign of the location of the victim, start probing the snow in the most likely burial areas with inverted ski poles, or, if they have been carried, probe poles. Probe the area below the last seen point. Look for natural entrapment areas such as trees, benches, the outer edge of corners of the avalanche path, and other areas of deposition.
- When the victim is found, treat for shock, suffocation, and cold.

Frostbite

Frostbite is one of the first hazards that come to mind when thinking of cold weather problems. Usually occurring in the extremities such as hands and feet and on the face, frostbite is the freezing of tissue due to exposure to cold. Wind, along with cold temperatures, increases the likelihood of frostbite. So will constrictive clothing such as tight mittens or boots.

Frostbite appears as a dull gray color on the skin. The victim first notices a numb sensation, then a deadness of feeling in the affected area.

Treatment of frostbite includes warming the affected part, if possible, in water 102 degrees to 105 degrees Fahren-heit. Avoid massaging or rubbing the injured area. Warming should only be carried out when the rescuers are certain that the victim will not be exposed to or can be protected from further cold.

Deal with frostbite as you would other winter hazards; prepare for it in advance. Bring adequate warm clothing that you've used and found reliable. If someone in the party gets cold feet or hands, stop immediately. Take a snack break and warm up the cold feet or hands against a volunteer's stomach. Going on could lead to serious problems. Besides, it feels good to put your cold feet on someone's stomach.

Warming cold feet on another's stomach.

Hypothermia

Injuries and Rescue

Hypothermia, another cold weather problem, is a lowering of the body temperature. Heat loss can occur through wet clothing, insufficient shielding from wind, a reduction (from inadequate food intake) of the energy reserves needed to keep the body warm in cool temperatures, and exhaustion.

The symptoms progress in stages: from feeling cold; to shivering; and then to uncontrollable shivering, stiff, jerky muscle movement, and poor coordination; and deteriorating to a stupor or dazed state. Death can, and does, occur in the later stage of hypothermia. Treatment includes immediately warming the victim by removing wet clothing and administering warm liquids. In extreme cases, the clothing of the victim should be removed and the victim should be immediately placed in a sleeping bag with an unclothed rescuer in an effort to bring the victim's body temperature back to normal.

There are, of course, a multitude of other first aid problems that can occur on ski trips including broken bones, cuts, and concussions. If you are involved in winter trips, you've probably already had solid background in first aid from summer trips. If not, take a Red Cross first aid course and learn the basics. Your time will be more than compensated when you have to deal with an injury.

If a serious injury occurs, stop and make camp. Warmth is very important in warding off shock in the injured person. Get any wet clothes off and immediately put the victim in a sleeping bag. While this is happening, the others can be readying camp, digging a snow cave or an igloo, or building a fire. Shock can be more severe in a wilderness setting and you need to make the victim comfortable.

Your party will then have to map out a plan. If there are two in your party, should you leave the injured person alone and go for help, or should you wait until he or she is stronger? If the injury is not serious, should you improvise a sled, or can the injured person continue skiing if his pack is divided among party members? Sleds can be made by lashing skis and poles together. Pads and packs can provide padding over the skis. Attach the rain-fly or a tent or a bivouac sack under the sled to make it easier to slide the sled. If it is up and down, hauling the sled can be impossible without more help and adequate equipment.

If a group of skiers finds itself in a dangerous location with an injured member of the party, *the group should not expect a rescue.*

Some skiers have a group of other experienced skiers and climbers on standby who will help if they have problems. But whatever the case, a distressed party should not expect others to risk their lives to save them. Sometimes help from an agency or organized county or provincial group is needed. A helicopter may be the only safe means of removing victims from a remote area.

Photographer's Notes

Many of the photographs in this book were taken during a ten-day skiing expedition across the new Gospel Hump Wilderness in central Idaho. Days are shorter in the winter, leaving less time for natural light shooting. If photography is the main objective of the expedition, it would be best to do your photographic work from a base camp, carrying only camera gear and lunch.

Warmth is clearly the key to productive shooting. If my feet or hands are cold, that is what I think about, not photographs. Good photographs require a lot of standing around waiting; waiting for the light to get right, for a skier to pass by, or for an animal to return. You should select your clothing for maximum warmth. Boots should be roomy enough for two pairs of socks, and felt liners. Fingered wool gloves are warmer than silk liners, and when combined with waterproof overmittens, solve the warmth/dexterity problem. My secret weapon was a hand warmer, which kept my hands, and my extra batteries, warm and functioning.

I chose my cameras for simplicity and light weight. I took two 35mm camera bodies (Canon F-1's), a 2X teleconverter, a small manual strobe, a light weight tripod with a ball head, a hand meter (Gossen Luna-Pro), a few filters (including a polarizing filter), and a lot of batteries. Don't take equipment totally dependant upon batteries. Cold batteries don't work well. Keep the extras close to your body for warmth. Alkaline power cells work best for cold weather.

I kept my cameras always cold in order to avoid the condensation which occurs when the camera is moved from warm to cold and vice-versa. An elastic strap, or Kuban hitch, around the body will hold your camera close to your chest when skiing. Advance and rewind your film slowly in order to avoid static electricity marks on your negatives.

I used Kodachrome 64 for color transparencies, from which high quality black and white prints (such as the one on page 78) can also be made, and Kodak Tri-X for black and white prints.

The skier/photographer might want to have waxless skis for greater maneuverability, lots of pockets in the pack for film and lenses, and a small belt pouch for a few rolls of film and a lens while on the trail.

Ron Watters is the Associate Coordinator of the Idaho State University Outdoor Program in Pocatello, Idaho. He is a certified cross-country ski instructor and guide, and most recently led the first winter crossing of the Gospel-Hump Wilderness, during which some of the photographs in this book were taken. He is the author of Ski Trails and Old-timers' Tales in Idaho and Montana *(Solstice Press, Moscow, Idaho 1978).*

Phil Schofield is a freelance photographer from Moscow, Idaho, who is the author/photographer of Portrait of the Palouse. *Recently, he has been doing work for the National Geographic Society, including the chapter on the Hell's Canyon in their* Majestic Canyons of America.

154